The Catering Management
HANDBOOK

The Catering Management HANDBOOK

The Complete Guide
to Hotel, Restaurant
and Outside Catering

Edited by
JUDY RIDGWAY
BRIAN RIDGWAY

KOGAN
PAGE

First published in 1994

Apart from any fair dealing for the purposes of research or private study, or criticism or review, as permitted under the Copyright, Designs and Patents Act, 1988, this publication may only be reproduced, stored or transmitted, in any form or by any means, with the prior permission in writing of the publishers, or in the case of reprographic reproduction in accordance with the terms of licences issued by the Copyright Licensing Agency. Enquiries concerning reproduction outside those terms should be sent to the publishers at the undermentioned address:

Kogan Page Limited
120 Pentonville Road
London N1 9JN

© Judy Ridgway and Brian Ridgway 1994

British Library Cataloguing in Publication Data

A CIP record for this book is available from the British Library.

ISBN 0–7494–0945–2

Typeset in Great Britain by Saxon Graphics Ltd, Derby
Printed and bound in Great Britain by Clays Ltd, St Ives plc

Contents

6

List of Contributors

William Bailey, MTS, HCIM, is an independent sales and marketing consultant in the catering industry. He has 25 years' experience, starting in operational management and then specialising in sales and marketing. He has worked with a number of well-known groups including Sonesta, Strand and Forte hotels. Until recently he was Group Marketing Director for Mount Charlotte Thistle Hotels.

Deborah Griffin, BSc, ACA, is a senior consultant for hotel and leisure consultants Pannell Kerr Forster Associates. Having qualified as a chartered accountant, she spent five years in the hotel industry. Deborah specialises in accounting, control and management information systems for hotels at PKFA.

Marion Hobbs is an independent design consultant specialising in hotel and restaurant design. She has 20 years' experience in the field. Clients have included Strand, Forte and De Vere hotels. She lectures on wall coverings and soft furnishings. She also has first-hand experience of designing and running her own restaurant.

Brian Mumford, BEM, is an independent security consultant specialising in hotel and catering work. He is connected with several large organisations. His past experience, which extends over 30 years, includes working for the government in the security field.

Brian Ridgway is Operations Director, London for the Mount Charlotte Thistle Hotels. He has 35 years of practical and line management experience in the hotel and catering industry including hotels and inns, outside catering, small satellite restaurants and exhibition catering.

Judy Ridgway, BA, is an author, journalist and broadcaster specialising in food, wine and catering. Her many books include *Running Your Own Catering Company* and *Running Your Own Wine Bar*. She has had first-hand experience of running her own catering company.

Chris Ripper, FHCIMA, FIPM, is Personnel and Trading Director of Scottish and Newcastle Retail. He has wide experience in the hospitality retail industry and has held senior personnel appointments in leisure retailing, hotels and latterly licensed house retailing.

Introduction

Judy Ridgway and Brian Ridgway

Almost everyone who works in catering dreams, at some time or another, of opening their own restaurant or running their own catering company. Graduates of the many craft and management courses, chefs and those who have made it on to the first steps of the management ladder may consider the notion in a more concrete form. For some the idea will be dismissed as unattainable or even as unwanted, but for others it will eventually blossom into a reality.

Running your own business is not for the faint-hearted, the mediocre or the disorganised. Careful planning, business acumen and real determination are required to turn a catering dream into a successful commercial operation.

Whether you are setting up a new company or taking over an existing business, either as owner/manager or as general manager, you will have to look at and make decisions on a whole host of areas which may not have come your way before.

In this handbook we aim to offer an *aide-mémoire* covering all the topics which must be considered, pointing the novice in the right direction, and reminding the more experienced manager of the many tasks to be undertaken when operating outside the umbrella of a large catering company with its band of experts at head office.

We cannot, in the space available, give every single answer or go into every detail – there are numerous books written about each of the main sections in this book – but we have brought all these subjects together in a single volume. We have also included what we hope will be useful checklists and a host of practical advice based on personal experience.

The contributors to this handbook are all experienced practitioners in their own fields. They have each used their own first-hand experience to highlight the most important areas to be explored in order to run a successful and profitable catering operation.

For more detailed information on any section consult the bibliography on page 235.

Part One

Setting Up

Judy Ridgway and Brian Ridgway

As well as understanding the principles of line management, the relevant legislation, accounting procedures, security and personnel management, the manager who wants to set up his or her own company must take into account a further dimension of requirements. It is not sufficient to have an idea about the type of restaurant or catering company you want to run; you must also be able to translate that vision into a convincing business plan and then make it work.

There is a vast difference between setting up your own catering business and working for someone else, so the first question is: do you have what it takes? Qualities required by anyone working in catering include:

- A liking for people in general
- A liking for and acceptance of long hours and hard work
- Good health
- The ability to cope with crises and mishaps without panicking
- The ability to accept criticism
- The ability to create all-round quality
- The ability to pay attention to detail
- The ability to resist the temptation to eat and drink too much.

Plus a professional approach to work. Additional qualities required by the new business entrepreneur include:

- A knowledge of the essentials
- Business acumen
- The ability to take risks
- Some creativity and original ideas
- Good organising ability
- The ability to work with others as equal partners or as boss
- Leadership qualities and the ability to train, motivate and discipline staff

- The ability to satisfy customer expectations
- A commitment to both customers and staff
- The ability to be flexible.

The last quality may be the one which is most put to the test in setting up a new business. In an ideal world your plan to open a genuine French bistro, a Spanish tapas bar or a catering company specialising in parties is worked out in some detail, premises are found in a suitable location, a name is chosen, a menu planned and the venture opens for business.

In practice it may be difficult to find the right kind of premises, the chosen location may be suffering economic or population changes or your financing may not be sufficient to buy the business you want. Your market research may indicate another kind of business more suited to a different type of customer or that you should start researching a different location altogether.

As well as being flexible, you must also be able to make a detached assessment of your aims, your product, your customers and your ability to deliver. This is essential whether you are starting up a new business or purchasing an existing one. Successful businesses (30 per cent of businesses fail within the first two years of trading) are those which research well, set careful plans and then make them happen.

Business Plans and Feasibilities

Deborah Griffin

The first step is to prepare a formal business plan. This should encompass full details of the product, be it restaurant, wine bar or catering company, pricing details, financing needs and clear objectives. The business plan is an essential document for obtaining funds from outside sources.

Information required

The following information needs to be determined and written down in detail in the preparation of the business plan. This formalisation of your ideas will also help to clarify in your own mind exactly what you are planning to do:

1 Aims: The aims of the business are closely tied in with your personal reasons for starting up or purchasing a business. There may be several aims such as running the best wine bar in town or running a successful outside catering company, but an essential consideration will be the minimum monetary return required by you.

2 Type of business: There are three main types of new business: sole trader, partnership and limited company, and each has its advantages and disadvantages (see pages 16–18).

3 The product: You will need to start working on a detailed outline of the kind of service you plan to offer. This will include details of the menu, the wine list and the prices. If the business is open to the public you will also need to consider the size and location of the premises and the ambience. Is there to be a special theme?

4 Customers: Whatever type of catering operation your business offers, identifying the right customers is critical (see page 25). How will you let them know you exist and persuade them to use your business? (See pages 177–183.)

5 Competition: The competition can be as important as the customers. It is important to know who they are, their strengths and weaknesses and who their customers are. Studying their success and failure may teach you valuable lessons. Establish whether there is a gap in the market, or whether you can provide the same service better or cheaper (see page 25). Remember that your success is likely to create similar competitors.

6 Personnel: Unless you are intending to be a sole trader with no employees, the abilities and personality of your partners and fellow directors, and your ability to recruit the right employees, could make the difference to the success of the business. Your ability to manage your employees will also be critical.

Checklist of the contents of a business plan

1. *Business details*
   - Name and trading address (see pages 19–20)
   - Type of business (see pages 16–18)
   - Proposed date of trading
   - Capital structure (if a limited company) or amount of capital provided (if a sole trader or partnership).
2. *Business objectives*
   - Strategy – how the objectives are to be achieved
   - Resources and methods to be used.
3. *Market information* (see page 25)
   - Your product/service
   - Size and location of the market
   - Seasonal demand and future growth prospects
   - Existing and potential customers
   - Existing and potential competition
   - Your marketing strategy (promotions, pricing, delivery etc) including costs involved (see pages 94–107 and 175–183).
4. *Suppliers*
   - Major suppliers and alternatives (see pages 113–116).
5. *Business premises and assets*
   - Details of freehold/leasehold premises (see pages 21–22)
   - For freeholds include valuation details and mortgages owed
   - For leaseholds include rents payable, rent review details, responsibility for repairs
   - Description of equipment owned or rented.
6. *Information about owners and managers*
   - Responsibilities of people involved in management, financial management, sales and marketing, and other key staff
   - Their particular skills, ages, qualifications and previous experience
   - Levels of their financial commitment.

7. *Detailed financial projections*
   - A profit forecast (see pages 51 and 54)
   - A cash flow forecast (see pages 50–51)
   - Balance sheet projections (sees pages 51 and 55)
   - Sensitivity analysis – what if sales fall by 20 or 30 per cent? (see pages 145–172)
   - Written report and explanation of plan.
8. *Detailed financial needs*
   - Total cost of project
   - Details of funding including grants, own resources etc.

Even if you intend to be a sole trader with no need to raise additional finance, it is good practice to write down most of the above details so that you can plan your future decisions.

1.2

Getting Organised

Deborah Griffin

At this stage you may wish to use professional advice. Certainly, you should establish relationships with certain people such as your bank manager, solicitor and accountant.

Professional advisers

Every business needs specialist legal and financial advice and if these specialists are appointed at an early stage they will be able to advise on all aspects of setting up the business, from deciding whether or not to buy a going concern to setting out budgets and forecasts and applying for a licence.

Take time over the choice and find out as much as you can before making a decision. An accountant does not need to be local to the business but it can be invaluable to use a local solicitor who will know what sort of attitude the local council has to planning applications and how the bench is likely to react to a licence application.

Most of the major banks have business advisers who go under various titles and whose brief it is to assist small businesses. Several also produce helpful (and free) books on starting a new business. Unless you already have a good relationship with your bank, you should shop around to find the type of assistance available and the terms of a business account.

An accountant is likely to be a very important person to your business, providing the advice that a financial director would normally provide. Accountants can assist with the preparation of business plans and cash flow forecasts, setting up and maintaining accounting records, handling taxation matters and advising on finance. As accountants can be costly it is essential that you get a good service. As with a bank you should shop around and not be afraid to demand a better service.

You should also make contact with the local authority, the tax office, and HM Customs and Excise for VAT registration. The local authority departments can be extremely useful with advice on requirements for trading licences, planning requirements and environmental health regulations. Your local authority may also have an economic development unit (or similar body) which will be helpful to any new business.

Many of these organisations produce leaflets on starting up a business and the various legal requirements. You may also consider commissioning a feasibility study of your proposals. This can help to gather the information required for the business plan, draw up the business plan and estimate potential profits and losses, cash flow requirements and returns. An independent feasibility study is often used to raise finance for larger projects such as a hotel or large restaurant.

Type of business

The next question is: what sort of business are you planning to run and what is its legal entity to be? The choice includes private ownership/sole trader, partnership or private limited company. Each method has its advantages and disadvantages. Consult your accountant and solicitor before making a final choice.

Sole trader

Advantages

- No legal formalities and you can start trading wherever and whenever it suits you
- You own the business yourself and answer to no one as to its management of profits
- You need no professional auditing so fees are minimised.

Disadvantages

- You are personally liable for all business debts, up to the limit of your financial capacity – which will include everything you own. Private backers may be used to find extra capital and if so they too will share the risk (or the profits).

Partnership

This is a firm with two or more proprietors. It is a joint venture based on mutual trust, in which each of the parties contributes something such as capital or specialised knowledge to start the business off and each shares in any profits that may result. There is no legal necessity for a formal written document drawn up by a solicitor, but it is in the interests of all the partners that one be adopted.

The most important feature of a partnership so far as the law is concerned is that each and every partner is an agent for the business and his or her action will be legally binding upon the other partners, unless such actions are outside the scope of the business. All parties are personally liable for the debts of all the partners.

Advantages

- You can bring together people with different skills which may help the business to be more viable
- No professional auditing is required so fees are minimised.

Disadvantages

- Each partner is personally liable for all the business's debts, on the same unlimited basis as a sole trader
- If a partner leaves the partnership or dies, his or her assets must be disposed of; this often leads to tax liabilities
- You are no longer the sole owner; each partner has a say about profits, share of the business and running of the business.

Private limited company

When a company is set up a new legal entity comes into being that is independent of the individuals who make up the company. A company can sue or be sued. It must have at least two shareholders, one director and a company secretary who can also be a director. The shareholders' liability for debt is limited to their shareholding but in practice banks and other lenders usually ask for personal guarantees against loans.

Before the company can be registered with the Registrar of Companies and granted a Certificate of Incorporation, those who wish to form the company must submit a Memorandum of Association and Articles of Association which set out what the company will be engaged in. Your solicitor will advise on this.

Alternatively, you can buy a company 'off the shelf' but you must be sure that the objects of the company you buy cover everything that you are likely to want to do now and in the future. Indeed, the wider the Memorandum and Articles are drafted the better.

Advantages

- You have no personal liability for any business debts
- You can raise capital by issuing shares in the company – the shareholders then own part of the company
- As a director you have all the benefits of an employee – NI contributions, unemployment benefit etc.

Disadvantages

- You must have an annual audit and your accounts must be available for public inspection
- Certain formalities are necessary before you start trading
- You must employ a company secretary and probably other directors
- You are under much tighter legal control.

1.3

The Product and Its Name

Brian Ridgway

The prospective restaurateur or caterer needs to have a clear idea of the kind of business he or she wants to run. What are its style and scope? Once this is clarified the basis will be there for planning the menus, planning the kitchen and service systems, looking for premises and finally moving on to the next stage of putting together a business proposal.

For the prospective restaurateur the kinds of question which need to be answered include:

- Town or country location, high street or side street, near competition or away from it?
- Fast food service or full service?
- Café, bistro or restaurant?
- Price, quality and image?
- Loud, buzzing atmosphere or quiet sophistication?
- Specialist food or ethnic?
- Ground floor, first floor or basement?
- Themed ambience or non-specific?
- Emphasis on the bar or the food?
- Age group or groups?
- Prospective size of the operation?
- Should there be an outline for further expansion once the business gets off the ground or is it a one-off?

For the private caterer the questions are less specific but it may still be useful to consider the various types of catering in which the company might specialise. These include:

Weddings and anniversaries
Children's events
Party catering in the home
Private outdoor catering and barbecues
Public event catering
Business functions and parties
Desk-top dining
Vegetarian or specialised catering
Frozen food service.

The picture which emerges with the answers to these questions is the ideal. In practice, market research may indicate a change of emphasis. Before any final decisions are made the prospective owner must look at the bill of fare and the style of service. The problem is that none of these things can be decided in isolation because each affects the other.

The menu, wine list and costings are covered in detail on pages 94–107.

The business will, of course, also have to have a name and the choice will need careful thought if it is to reflect the nature of the product on offer. You should by now be quite clear about what kind of restaurant or catering company you want to run and so should try to choose a name which will be in keeping.

Ideally, the name should be original, attractive, easy to remember and say, and convey sufficient interest for the customer to want to find out more. Take time in deciding on the name for it will not be that easy to change it.

The name must create the right sort of image for the business. A grand name may well discourage customers looking for something cheap and cheerful whereas the use of a slang expression may not be appropriate for an upmarket restaurant. Caterers will also want to inspire confidence among potential clients.

Some names lend themselves better to the development of a marque or logo and this should be discussed with a graphic designer.

Your local Companies Registration Office provides two booklets: 'Business Names – Guidance Notes' and 'Company Names – Guidance Notes'. These tell you what you are allowed to use without permission and the regulations you must comply with if you are going to trade under a name which is not your own. Companies, or where the name chosen is not your own, must make sure that there will be no objection to the chosen name, for example by a business with a similar name. Failure to do so could cost a great deal of money.

On the other hand, you may give extra protection to the name you have chosen so that no one else can use it. This can be done with trademark registration.

The name of the business together with other information such as permanent address and names of co-directors must be on all business letterheads, invoices, receipts and so on. Companies Registration Offices also produce examples.

Location and Premises

Brian Ridgway

Location is, of course, extremely important. All businesses must be near potential customers but this may be less important for an outside catering company than for a restaurant or wine bar. Caterers can travel to their customers and low rents may be more important. The premises will only be used for preparation and storage and the customer is unlikely to see them. However, the business should be reasonably accessible for supplies and deliveries and be within reach of an appropriate labour force.

As well as being near potential customers, many restaurants and wine bars need to have a reasonable passing trade. One way to check on a potential site is to see if there is a McDonald's, Marks & Spencer or Pizza Hut in the area. These organisations have done their market research and know the good sites. The only other way is to stand and count the people passing by. This should be done at potentially quiet times as well as at rush hours or peak shopping times.

A decision must also be made whether or not to be in the same location as the competition. This can be good idea because potential customers are already going to the area. But it may be better for certain types of business to be on their own.

In practice the business may have to open in a compromise location and it will then be important to make the most of the good points and minimise the bad ones. Create attractive, visible signs and make access as easy as possible. Remember that local directional signs to a catering outlet in a side street or down country lanes may need planning permission.

The actual buying decision will be governed not only by location but also by the type of premises required.

Freehold or leasehold?

The following points need to be taken into consideration when making this decision:

Freehold

- Normally an appreciating asset (1989–1993 excepted)
- No consents required from the leaseholder; you are your own boss
- Attractive to purchasers in the future and easier to dispose of, if necessary
- Borrowing from the bank will be easier.

Leasehold

- Generally a declining asset, particularly in later years as the number of years outstanding diminishes
- More difficult to borrow from the bank as the property is harder to dispose of
- Consents will be required from the lessor
- Extra cost involved in rents or ground rents.

Leasehold can be a useful short-term solution for preparation and storage units for a catering company but not so good for a restaurant wishing to build up loyalty and goodwill.

Under the Town and Country Planning Acts 1971 (and their Scottish equivalents) there is a good deal of official control over the use to which the land and property are put. Power is vested in each local planning authority and it is the duty of this authority to ensure that all land and property in its area is used for the best possible purposes in the light of the shortage of land and the needs of the community.

Planning permission is not usually required for internal alterations which do not change the use to which the building has been put and which do not materially change the appearance of the building. If the premises are licensed, plans for any alteration may have to be submitted to the licensing justices.

If major alterations are envisaged, it is advisable to check with the local authority with regard to planning, fire prevention, environmental health and, if the premises are able to be licensed, with the Clerk to the Licensing Court.

Taking Over a Going Concern

Brian Ridgway

One of the first questions to consider once the decision to set up a business has been taken is whether or not to buy a going concern.

The advantages of buying an existing business are that it will require less capital than starting up from scratch, it will probably take less time to find a good location and the existing business can be studied in detail before a commitment is made. Once a business has been found the new company can take over and start up straightaway.

The disadvantages are that you may not find exactly what you want and even if you do the business may not be in very good shape. Indeed, it is worth finding out why the existing owner is selling. It could be that local unemployment is rising or that the area is changing in such a way that the business will be affected in the future.

Before making a decision carry out market research (see page 25). Then ask all the questions that you would ask when buying a house plus the following:

- Is what you want to do right for the area and the premises?
- Why is the business being sold and does the answer make sense?
- Check out the condition of the mechanical and electrical equipment. How long will it last?
- Check the last six years' accounts.
- Check the number of staff employed, the wages, services agreements and any other commitments.
- Is the business registered for VAT? Watch for operations which have not been declaring their sales to the VAT inspector and the Inland Revenue.
- What fixtures and fittings are/are not for sale? Ask for lists.
- Don't appear too eager.

The price of the business will take in the property and might well include the fixtures and fittings. Sometimes a going concern will also ask for a fee for its goodwill but it is wise to be sceptical of exaggerated claims to a fund of long-standing customers. There is no guarantee that they exist or if they do that they will continue to come to the restaurant or order catering services after a change of ownership.

When agreeing a price it makes sense to agree an inventory too. Check the condition of the furniture, glass, china and cutlery and make sure that antiques do not disappear into thin air once the sale has been agreed.

If a licence is involved it should be a condition of the sale that the licence is satisfactorily transferred.

Other points to consider:

- Have the owners taken bookings to which you will be committed and, if so, are they properly costed?
- Don't pay more than the previous owner paid for contracted goods and services and don't pay VAT again.
- Check that the age of stock is well within the 'use by' date. Check that it is all in good condition.
- Check outstanding debtors and creditors.

Do not spend all your preliminary budget on the purchase of the property and fittings – you will need to keep some of it for expenses until you start to generate cash flow from ongoing sales.

Once the takeover is complete the following organisations will need to be informed:

Environmental Health Office – registration and check
Customs and Excise – VAT
Inland Revenue – tax
Data Protection Register
Local Council Rating Department – Council Tax
Licensing Authority to apply for a licence.

Market Research

William Bailey

Market research is concerned with looking at business opportunities and with investigating the marketplace in which the business is to operate. It will cover the following points:

- What is the competition doing and how successful are they?
- Is there a potential demand for the specific package planned? If not, is there another untapped niche market in the area?
- What type of customer is available – business people who are likely to entertain or eat out themselves, tourists, visitors to special events, residents of upmarket flats and houses who do a lot of home entertaining or go out a lot? Is there likely to be any change in the profile now or in the future?
- What is the age and the disposable income of the prospective customers?
- Is there car parking?
- Are there any hidden pitfalls in the area such as a change in local regulations? Could the area be made a pedestrian precinct? Is there to be road widening? Might you lose the car park?
- Is there any possibility of a change of emphasis to another part of town which will then attract custom from your chosen site? Is the area dependent on any large businesses that could be in danger of moving or slimming down?
- Are there local pressure groups who will oppose the opening of the business?
- Will there be objections from residents in the area to late evening parking and banging of car doors?
- Will there be any problems in getting a licence?

This research will, it is hoped, have been undertaken with an open mind. Do not use research with the objective of satisfying your own views. Instead, compare the results of unbiased market research to your ideal plan and if the two do not match make changes as necessary or start looking in another area.

Finding the Money

Deborah Griffin

There are many different sources of finance. Correct advice and guidance is important to ensure that your business obtains the best deal. The main types of finance available are: government assistance, equity – internal and external, and borrowing.

Government assistance

This is a vital area of consideration for the small business. There are many different schemes available; most are discretionary and depend on the business demonstrating that the project would not go ahead in its present form without government support. Therefore this should be one of the first sources of finance investigated. Assistance may depend on the type of business and its location. As well as grants, free or subsidised advisory and consultancy support may also be available. Your local government economic development unit or Local Enterprise Agency should be able to help you.

Equity

Equity represents the owner's interests in the business and may simply be the capital belonging to you and your partners. Other individuals and institutions may also provide capital in expectation of a return in the form of dividends on their shares and involvement in the management of the business. Such involvement may include voting rights on the appointment of directors or representation on the board of directors. Principal sources of equity are:

- Relatives, friends and individuals
- Development capital groups, such as 3i
- Venture capital and specialist investment institutions
- Equity divisions of clearing banks
- Merchant banks

- The Stock Exchange
- Investment trust companies
- Pension funds
- Insurance companies
- Certain public sector agencies.

Most small businesses will be of little interest to equity financiers. Generally, the funds to be extended will need to be larger than most small businesses require. Venture capitalists normally require that the returns should show significant growth potential. In some cases there must be the possibility of a market for the shares within the medium term.

Most equity for a small business will come from the owners and their friends and relatives. The relationship between the amount of equity and borrowing in the business is known as *gearing*, and may be expressed in the form of a gearing ratio. The gearing ratio is often used by lending institutions, such as banks, to calculate borrowing limits.

These limits are important to the lenders to ensure that their security is covered in the case of the business's failure and that interest payments will be met. Conversely, it is important to ensure that your business is not too highly geared (excessive borrowing in relation to equity), so that interest and debt repayments are covered by earnings and cash flow is available. To avoid undue strain there are two rules of thumb:

- Trading profits before interest and tax should be three times the annual interest charge
- A gearing ratio of 1 to 1 (ie equal amounts of debt and equity) indicates a sound balance sheet.

Borrowing

Borrowings need not be permanent and are generally repayable, either on demand or in a predetermined schedule. Interest is usually paid to the lenders and offset against the profits of the business, so reducing the tax to be paid. Lenders will usually require security in the form of debentures over business assets and occasionally personal guarantees, where the owner's personal assets are at risk in the event of business failure.

Borrowing may be classified into short term, medium term and long term. Another important rule of thumb is to match the term of borrowing with the useful life of the assets being financed.

Short-term borrowings up to one year are usually required to bridge seasonal variations when receipts and payments do not match or to finance items such as stock which will be converted into cash fairly quickly. Common types of short-term borrowings are:

- Bank overdrafts
- Debt factoring where a company takes on your debts paying you a percentage of the total
- Invoice discounting to encourage quicker payment by customers

- Taking extended credit from suppliers
- Bill finance.

Medium-term borrowings from one to five years are more often used to finance the purchase of equipment or machinery or general working capital. Common types of medium-term borrowings which usually require security are:

- Medium-term bank loans
- Hire purchase and instalment credit
- Finance leases
- Operating leases
- Debentures.

Long-term borrowings over five years are used to purchase land, buildings or major plant with a long useful life, and to acquire other businesses. Common types of long-term borrowing are:

- Long-term bank loans
- Mortgages
- Sales and lease-back deals
- Debenture/loan stocks.

If you have an existing business you should examine it to see if you can find the capital you require from within the business itself before you borrow funds from external sources.

Checklist of dos and don'ts of raising finance

In starting up your business it is likely that you will require more than one type of finance. Before you decide on the kind of financial package to seek, consider these dos and don'ts.

Do

- Check the terms and conditions of any loans offered to you, particularly with regard to committing your personal assets to unlimited guarantees.
- Ensure that your business has adequate financial controls to provide accurate management information to keep you up to date with exactly how the business is performing.
- Keep the lender informed of how your business is progressing to gain and retain his or her confidence.
- Make a detailed assessment of your financial needs and allow a margin for error.
- Aim to achieve a manageable gearing ratio.

Don't

- Try to borrow from too many sources or play one financier off against another.

- Take on unmanageable commitments which cannot be covered by the cash flow of the business.
- Refuse to part with equity or give reasonable security as evidence of your personal commitment – either could limit your opportunities.

1.8

Insurance

Brian Ridgway

It is advisable to discuss insurance needs in detail with a reputable insurance broker. Ask for competitive quotes from the recommended insurance companies.

You may need insurance cover for the following:

- Employer's liability
- Public liability
- Buildings
- Delivery vehicles
- Contents including stock
- Loss of cash
- Glass
- Loss of profits after a fire or other accident.

Additional insurance might also be needed for:

- Personal accident and sickness for all staff
- Freezer contents and frozen food
- Small computers
- Expenses on legal disputes

- Goods in transit
- Bad debts
- Loss of licence
- Failure of vital services
- Fidelity insurance
- Key man insurance – if your partner were to die you might need to buy his or her share to keep control of the business.

Whatever the insurance that you decide to take, make sure that there are no high excess clauses. Arrange to pay monthly to help your cash flow.

It is important to review the degree of risk associated with each potential policy. Apart from the insurance which is legally required for the business you are actually purchasing expensive 'peace of mind' policies. Some of the policy costs may well exceed the amount you are normally likely to have to pay in the event of a problem and it might be better to set aside a disaster fund instead.

Registration and Licence

Brian Ridgway

The new food hygiene laws require you to register with the local environmental health office before you open the business. This applies to catering companies as well as to restaurants.

Applying for a licence

The modern licensing laws are governed by Licence Act 64 Section 8(4) and the Licensing (Scotland) Act 1976 which both deal with the sale of intoxicating liquor.

In England and Wales there is a standard procedure for applying for all types of justices' licence and written notice must be given at least 21 days before the hearing of the licensing justices to the Clerk of the Court, the local chief officer of police, the appropriate local authority and the administration officer of the local fire service. The copy to the Clerk of the Court must be accompanied by a plan of the premises.

During the 28-day period prior to the date of the hearing the applicant must display a copy of his or her notice of intended application on or near the premises to be licensed in a place where it can easily be read by the public. It must remain there for seven days.

In the period of 28 to 14 days before the hearing, the applicant must publish a copy of the application in the local newspaper circulating in the district.

All these notices may be made on standard forms supplied by the Clerk to the Justices on request.

In Scotland, applications are made on a prescribed form completed and signed by the applicant or his or her agent and must be lodged with the Clerk to the licensing board not later than five weeks before the sitting together with the plans if it is a new certificate. The notice must be displayed at the premises at least 21 days before the hearing and it must be published in a local newspaper not later than two days before the hearing.

It is advisable to consult with the Clerk to the Justices, the local authority and the chief of the local fire prevention unit before plans are finalised or the application is made to ensure that they are likely to agree to the application without any last-minute, unforeseen hitches. In any case, full cooperation with all the authorities involved is the wisest course of action and generally you will find them most helpful.

Licensing can be handled by yourself but it is advisable, if it is the first time, to engage the services of a reliable licensing solicitor who will take over the responsibility for a fee.

1.10

Creating the Kitchen Systems and Service Planning

Brian Ridgway

The kitchen systems and service plan is usually worked out by experienced owner/ managers or by the chef but it is possible to get a considerable amount of detailed advice either from a general catering equipment supplier who has a whole range of equipment for sale or from individual catering equipment manufacturers. The latter will probably expect you to buy their equipment which may not suit you, or for a fee you can engage the services of an independent consultant.

The plan must take in:

- The hygiene of the kitchen.

- The general and specific layout of the kitchen, service and cleansing areas, and the provision of an office or administration area for the head chef.
- The equipment which will be required.
- The expected work pattern and flow.

Hygiene

Consult the local Environmental Health Officer with detailed plans and layouts before making any final decisions. This will eliminate the risk of having to make changes at a later date. It also sets up a useful working liaison with the Environmental Health Department and environmental health officers will appreciate the fact that their help and advice were sought from the beginning.

Good hygiene practices are extremely important (see page 133) and the standards laid down by law (see pages 71–73) must be instituted and maintained at all times. These include regulations on the construction of the kitchen and the materials used as well as on the siting and number of various types of equipment such as sinks, washbasins, fridges and chilling equipment.

Kitchen area

The kitchen can be split up in different ways, depending upon the size of the operation. A small restaurant or catering company might divide the kitchen into two areas – preparation and kitchen service. The preparation area will be used for the preparation of vegetables, fish, meat and poultry as well as desserts, cold starters, salads and decorative work. The kitchen service area will be the cooking area and plating or serving area.

Larger establishments will split preparation areas into meat, fish and vegetable preparation and split the cooking and service area into sections or corners specialising in different methods of cooking or preparation, such as soups, fish cooking, entrée cooking, roasting and grilling, vegetables and potato cooking, sweets and larder where the raw and cold preparation takes place.

Here is a checklist to use when creating or refurbishing the kitchen:

- *Ceiling:* should be easily cleaned
- *Walls and woodwork:* make sure that there are no hidden interstices or panelling which could harbour dust or vermin. Must be easy to clean
- *Floor:* should be made of impervious and durable material which is easy to keep clean. It should also be non-slip
- *Lighting:* must reach a minimum of 400lux at working level
- *Ventilation:* window extractors or ventilation and a canopy over the hob are essential. The siting of fridges, freezers and coolers should also be checked as they can all give off heat
- *Electrics:* make sure that there are sufficient points for all the equipment to be installed. Check for over-loading
- *Work surfaces:* must be impervious and washable
- *Washing facilities:* in addition to the preparation and washing-up sinks there must be separate washbasins for staff and separate sanitary accommodation supplied

- *Plumbing*: appliances such as refuse disposal units and potato peelers must be plumbed in and the pipes inspected to see that they will clear properly.

Workflow

The kitchen layout must be planned for the most efficient movement of people and goods.

- Chefs have to be able to work in a logical way on a stove with a work station and fridges close by and be able to deliver the food to the service hot plate without having to walk for miles or get in anyone else's way.
- It must be possible to move goods easily into bulk storage areas on arrival in the building and then from storage to preparation areas.
- In a restaurant the waiting staff need to be able to drop dirty china, cutlery and glasses on entering the servery area. They also need to go on to place an order or pick up an order to take to a customer in such a way that they do not interfere with the kitchen staff or the kitchen staff with them. They should not have to double back on themselves or move into the path of other waiting staff behind them.

Storage space (see also pages 125–127)

Outside the kitchen area there must also be space for:

- Bulk storage of frozen and chilled foods
- Dry goods storage
- Vegetable storage
- Equipment storage
- Waste disposal containers.

And outside the restaurant, space will be required for:

- Storage of linen, china, cutlery, glasses and small items of equipment
- Storage of wine and liquor
- Hanging space for staff uniforms, changing rooms and toilets
- Storage of cleaning materials, brooms, mops, vacuum cleaners and polishes
- Storage of hazardous materials such as chemical solutions for cleaning.

Administration area

The chef needs an administrative area or office where he can work and store the appropriate paperwork to carry out his administrative responsibilities. This will include buying specifications; suppliers' lists; price call-over sheets and copy order sheets (see pages 108–122); as well as standard recipes, perhaps with photographs and costings (see pages 94–107), party or function menus for the week; kitchen rotas and wage authorisation sheets. There must also be a notice board for statutory notices.

Equipment

The menu and the number of customers expected will dictate the detail of the equipment required but the list is likely to include the following:

Cooking

Ovens: for roasting, braising and baking should be well insulated, have an even temperature distribution and be easy to clean. Microwave or combination ovens should be heavy duty models.
Solid tops and burners
Grills
Deep fat fryers: ideally a kitchen should have three, one each for fish, meat and vegetables. Look for equipment with the latest safety controls.
Brat pans, pans, steamers and stock pots
Chopping and cutting boards
Utensils

Keeping food hot

Hot cupboards, fixed or mobile
Plate lowerators, fixed or mobile
Bains-maries

Water

Water heaters
Coffee makers
Water boilers

Cold storage

Refrigerators and freezers: preferably with instant cooling systems which come into operation when the doors are opened
Check defrosting and cleaning systems as well as capacity and fuel consumption
Blast chillers and cold storage shelves for fast cooling prior to freezing

Washing up

Sinks: double or treble sinks for the separate washing of foods, dishes and hands.
Dishwashers: there is now a wide variety of dishwashers available designed to cope with different types of restaurant with different volumes of customers. The larger dishwashers work on a continuous flow basis where the grids of cutlery and rack of plates are continuously fed in at one end and will emerge at the other efficiently cleaned, sterilised and dried. There are also semi-manual machines similar to but stronger than a domestic dishwasher.
Pan washing machines are also available, but most pans need to be scoured first.
If dishwashers or glasswashers are being used there is a statutory requirement for a temperature of 77°C (170°F) to sterilise or for appropriate chemicals to be used.
Cleaning equipment for EPNS.

Knives are not usually provided as each chef should have his own personal set, but it might be necessary to have a few common knives for general use or to lend to apprentices who are just starting.

1.11

Creating the Ambience

Marion Hobbs

The menu, the name, the design, the decor, the furniture, the lighting, the accessories, the signs, the uniforms, the tableware, the music and not least the staff, together play an integral part in creating the ambience.

In order to determine the ambience you wish to create it is essential to refer to your detailed notes on:

- The type of operation, service and name
- The customers – their needs, price range and expectations
- The menu with a basic outline of the type of food and the presentation
- The number of covers
- The position of the kitchen, bar, servery counters, entrance and fire exits and the workflow
- The budget.

This will help to clarify what you are offering the customer and therefore the requirements of the design. It will enable a brief to be written which can be used either by outside consultants or by whoever is in charge of planning and purchasing.

The right consultants can ease your way through the minefield of legislation. They also offer creativity, experience and project management. The latter can include advice on the form of building contracts such as tender, design and build. Consultants can negotiate for you and coordinate all disciplines to create a total ambience.

Consultants must be cost-effective and sympathetic to your needs and what you wish to achieve. There must be strong cost control without crushing the design and ambience. It is your money they are spending.

It is important to establish a realistic budget early on. To achieve this, produce a separate budget for each area such as the restaurant, the bar, the offices and kitchen, allowing for the following:

- Specialist consultants: including architects, structural engineers, heating ventilation engineer, interior designer, kitchen consultant, graphic designer
- Graphics: including a logo, external and internal signing, menus, bills and promotional material
- Building works: including electrics, plumbing, damp-proof course, structural work, heating and ventilation
- Design: including shopfitting, finishes, furnishings, fittings and equipment, lighting and accessories
- Uniforms, tableware and sundry equipment.

Then go on to produce sample boards of the schemes for each area. These should include all materials and paint colours, photos of furniture and light fittings with references, sources and a schedule of costs. This will prove invaluable as an ongoing guide throughout the project. Make sure that the appropriate board is updated should any changes occur. At the completion of the project check that all boards are an accurate 'as built' reference. This will provide useful information for future maintenance and re-orders.

If an unforeseen occurrence demands that the budget has to be altered, remember, before making any major alterations, that interference with the visual impact could produce a negative reaction. This sector of the budget should be adequately funded at all times.

The design of the restaurant

The design should be an effective sales tool and achieve a happy balance between function and aesthetics. The success of a good interior is one that is not only cost-effective but continues to look fresh and attractive after continual use.

The first impression is the one that lasts. The initial impact sets the mood of the customer. The entrance to a high street restaurant is usually a plate glass door, so it is easy to see beyond the threshold and inside. If the customer cannot see in there is a psychological barrier which may put people off stepping over the threshold into the unknown. This barrier must be minimised.

The exterior and interior should both consist of good use of colour, materials and lighting with innovative signing. The mix should draw the customer to venture within. The lasting impression should be fresh, original, inviting, attractive and personable with attentive, enthusiastic staff and good food!

All materials need to be hard wearing, require little maintenance and must comply with the local fire officer's requirements. The materials need not be expensive. A strong ambience can be achieved with a good use of colour, a creative use of lighting and striking accessories.

Wall coverings: There is a wide range of alternatives from wallpapers, smooth or rough textured plaster, plain painted walls to walls with different paint techniques such as ragroll or *trompe-l'oeil*, to exclusive silks, tapestries and other textures.

An extensive range of attractive wall coverings in a contract quality now exists. Be wary of using domestic papers. These materials may look subtle and sophisticated in a living room but soon appear jaded in a constant working environment.

Examples of hard wall finishes include timber, tiles, steel, glass and marble.

Soft furnishings: There is now an abundance of materials available. The manufacturer or designer can advise whether the chosen materials are suitable for their purpose. Points to check are: abrasion tests, colour fastness, durability, vulnerability to stains, and wear and tear.

All materials must comply with the local fire officer's requirements. This includes nets, curtains, linings, trimmings, upholstery materials and fillings.

Another important point is whether the materials will withstand washing or whether they will have to be dry cleaned. The correct cleaning process for all materials must be checked so that the fire retardancy will not be affected.

If curtains are a predominant part of the scheme, it is better to spend money on an effective curtain treatment such as swags, tails and blinds, rather than relying on just the fabric design. A similar effect may be achieved by using dress curtains rather than going to the expense of operating curtains.

Flooring: A wide range of flooring finishes is available such as carpet, timber, tiles, marble and terrazzo. Points to consider are wear, tear and maintenance. If carpet is used it needs to be of a contract quality with a good quality underlay. Skilful use of colour and design will help the carpet to stay looking fresh.

Remember the vulnerable places such as heavy traffic areas, entrances, cloakrooms and areas adjacent to the kitchens. The manufacturer or designer can advise on the appropriate finish and maintenance of each area.

Fittings: Bar counter, reception counter, servery, menu stand, banquette seating, service stations, screens, column and dado rails; all these need careful consideration and will only be successful if they meet the needs of the restaurant ergonomically and functionally. They could well be the most expensive items in the scheme. The designer will therefore need an accurate brief concerning operation and usage.

Time spent planning the layout of the furniture, serving and service elements is crucial. Consideration should be given to:

- The staff movement between the guests and the kitchens
- The proximity of the tables, servery counters and service stations to the kitchens
- The noise level
- The guests' view of the kitchens.

The positioning of the fixed items is critical. Bad positioning could be costly and jeopardise the whole operation. The positioning of these items could affect any changes you may wish to make in the future. Good workmanship and hard-wearing materials are essential. Keep entrances and fire exits free. The layout should be adaptable to accommodate the number of covers and use, and possible revised layouts in the future.

Loose furniture: When choosing loose furniture consider the ease of movement to give flexibility, the stability of the tables, and the shape and size. When using chairs with arms check that they can be drawn up to the table without the arms hitting the edge of the table. Where vulnerable edges are upholstered make sure that an appropriate material is used.

Lighting: This is an important aspect of the design. The impact of a successful interior and exterior is enhanced by the imaginative use of lighting. The quality and effect of the lighting will establish the ambience which can be soft, hard, dramatic, theatrical, intense, functional, highlight or pinpoint. Lighting is an area where you should not attempt to skimp on costs.

The lighting must relate to the layout. Once the level of lighting is achieved make sure that your staff are aware of the correct level and if using dimmers mark the appropriate levels accordingly. The whole effect can be ruined by setting the lighting at the wrong level.

Graphic design

First, the *design or logo* of the name of the company or restaurant must be strong and consistent. Use it on all the company's promotional material including menus, letterheads, bills, brochures, signs and logos.

Whatever kind of catering outlet you are running your *menu* is your shop window and your branding. For a catering company it is your only shop window.

Customers should be immediately aware of the menu and respond instantaneously. They should be enticed in by a restaurant menu and want to find out more. They should be tempted to expand their ideas by an exciting catering menu.

In a restaurant the menu must be positively and attractively displayed, externally as well as internally. A professionally printed menu looks good and inspires confidence but printing costs can be expensive and this tends to inhibit regular changes in the menu.

If the budget is tight it is worth considering a more flexible approach such as handwriting or word processor printout. This kind of flexible menu allows for experiment and change, particularly in the first months. A restaurant or wine bar may use a blackboard but this must be consistent with the atmosphere.

Another method is to have the main structure of the menu printed with a space for inserts such as a handwritten entry or a slip of paper attached with a clip. It is important that any additions or attachments to the menu are an integral part of the design and do not appear as an after-thought. Whichever method is chosen a clear brief should be provided.

Some of these methods will also be appropriate for outside catering companies but their menus will probably need to be much more flexible. Some companies work solely from a wide range of set menus but it is worth considering some element of individual planning.

Customers like to feel that they are receiving a tailor-made service. This can be achieved by offering to mix-and-match from existing menus or by showing sample menus and building a brand new menu on the basis of discussion with the client. The latter method will take more time but this can be costed into the prices quoted.

Menus can be sent out alone but they will have much more impact if they are sent out as part of a company brochure. Like the menu, the brochure should be carefully designed to create the right image of the company and its services.

The design of the *wine list* is also important. Here again a printed list adds authority but it can be expensive to keep reprinting every time a particular wine changes vintage or runs out. On the other hand nothing looks worse than a printed wine list with handwritten changes. Doing nothing is even more annoying to customers when they find that what they ordered is not available.

Some restaurants try to get round this by leaving the details of the vintages off the list altogether, but customers who know their wines want to know exactly what is on offer. Generally speaking, it is better to give as much information as possible about a wine. However, this information must be factual – vintage, producer, negociant, bottler or shipper – not flowery and possibly inaccurate descriptions of the wine.

Consider a more modern approach and classify your wines by grape variety rather than by country or region of origin. Many wine lovers have reached their level of enjoyment through the New World wines which nearly always use varietal labelling and people understand it.

Extensions to the overall design

Uniforms, tableware, food presentation and sundry equipment are essential extensions of the overall design and ambience.

Uniforms: These should be suitable for both sexes and for all shapes and sizes. They should also be easy to maintain and above all be a pleasure to wear! Nobody will perform their job well if they feel uncomfortable and detest what they are expected to wear every day. Remember, your staff are a very important part of the ambience of the restaurant and need to be involved, preferably from the start.

Table tops: The choice includes polished tops with mats, marble, pine, laminates or table cloths with matching napkins or paper. The choice will depend upon the type of restaurant. If table cloths are chosen, linen (though initially more expensive) is superior to cotton which creases and soils easily. Other choices include paper, plastic or oilcloth. Cloths with slips (two cloths of different size) save money. Six sets of napkins will be required per cover with a further 20 per cent to cover loss or damage.

Crockery: The choice includes vitreous china, hotelware (hardwearing), metallised bone china (attractive but expensive). Vitrified earthenware is not so attractive but cheap. Badged or monogrammed cutlery and china cuts down on pilfering.

Serving dishes: The choice includes metalware with lids, ovals and rounds. Aluminium is not acceptable; stainless steel is strong but expensive. Electroplated nickel silver (EPNS) is attractive but expensive and also needs to be cleaned.

Most of these considerations are peculiar to restaurants but some catering companies also stock up with all their own glasses, serving dishes, crockery and cutlery. This ensures continuity but at least in the early stages it will probably make more sense to keep your capital fluid and use an equipment hire company. Build up a good relationship with one or two companies.

The design of the bar

The design of the bar should be in keeping with the design of the restaurant because it is important that the two areas complement one another.

The bar is usually best sited near the entrance to a restaurant so that all customers pass it. Make sure that there are enough seats for customers to enjoy a drink while perusing the menu and giving their orders. This activity should be as visual as possible to encourage other guests to follow suit. Whether or not the bar is visible from the street will depend upon the required atmosphere of the establishment. An adjacent cloakroom is useful so that bar staff can help with coats as necessary.

Outside caterers too should set up a pay bar near the entrance to a marquee or the food service area. Non-pay bars may be better sited away from the entrance to avoid congestion.

A restaurant bar should be professionally planned with a good visual display and plenty of back-up storage. The same considerations as those given to the design of the restaurant will also apply here. In addition, running hot and cold water must be laid on. There must also be a good working surface, chilling units and glass storage. Provision must be made for ice.

Other equipment includes the telephone and till. Both these may serve the restaurant as well as the bar, and if they do the bar staff will need a reservations book so that they can double as reservations takers.

Apart from the obvious items such as corkscrew, crown cork opener and sharp knife, the most important items on the bar are the measures. These must conform to legal standards (see page 141).

It is tempting to have the correct glass for every drink but this is not only expensive but can take up too much valuable space in the bar. A simple restaurant bar could probably manage with four different glasses: all-purpose goblets for wines, aperitifs and spirits, tumblers for water or spirits and mixers, beer glasses and liqueur glasses.

However, the more sophisticated the restaurant, the more customers will expect certain drinks to be served in particular glasses and at the very least you will need to add champagne flutes, brandy glasses and port glasses.

In some bars the bar staff are also responsible for glass washing and so a glass washing machine will be required (see page 35). Site this out of sight of the customers, behind the bar or in an adjacent room.

Part Two

Financial Accounts and Budgetary Control

Deborah Griffin

Recording Income and Expenditure

Deborah Griffin

Whether you are a small self-employed caterer working from home or the owner of a restaurant, it is essential that you have an effective bookkeeping system to record all expenditure and income related to the business. This is required for tax purposes (both income tax and VAT) but will also help you to manage the business by providing information on the following when you need it:

- *Cash position*: many small businesses fail through lack of cash even though they are making profits
- *Debtors and creditors*: this is linked to the cash position in that sales made need to be transferred into cash and creditors' payments met regularly
- *Variable costs*: the margins you are achieving need to be monitored to ensure that pricing is correct and your objectives met
- *Overhead costs*: with margins achieved, the level of overheads will determine the amount of sales you need to break even
- *Stock levels*: when compared to the level of sales this will indicate whether stock levels are optimised
- *Profits*.

It is important that you write down the transactions your business is incurring regularly. Once set up, it is not difficult to maintain a simple system of accounts. Usually the accounts will be physical books but alternatively you may wish to use one of the many standard computer bookkeeping packages available.

The following books are those which you should always consider keeping.

Cash book

Even the simplest business set-up will need to maintain a cash book. This simply records cash received and expended. Columns can also provide an analysis of the

SIMPLE CASH BOOK FOR CASH BUSINESSES

CASH RECEIVED

DATE	DETAIL	INV NO/REF	BANK	VAT	FOOD	BEVERAGE	TOBACCO	ETC
1.1	BALANCE B/F		569.00					
1.1	TAKINGS		456.00	67.9	346.23	32.7	9.2	
2.1	TAKINGS		326.45	48.60	222.12	55.7		
TOTAL FOR MONTH								
BALANCE C/F								

CASH EXPENDITURE

DATE	DETAIL	CHQ NO/REF	TOTAL	VAT	SALARIES	FOOD	BEVERAGE	TOBACCO	DRAWINGS	ETC
1.1	XYZ LTD	233	109.00	16.20		92.80				
	PETTY CASH	234	100.00							100
2.1	CASH	235	200.00						200	
	SALARIES	236	85.00		85.00					

income and expenditure. If you are registered for VAT there should always be a VAT column for both income and expenditure.

Income columns may analyse receipts by type of business such as food, wines and beers. Expenditure columns should provide an analysis of variable costs such as food and beverage, and overhead costs such as rent, insurance and energy costs. Where there are sales on credit, income received may be entered into two columns – cash and accounts receivable (see 'Sales day book' below).

All columns should be totalled at least monthly. The difference between the cash receipts and cash expended is the bank balance (after allowing for any items to be cleared through the banking system). You may need to enter items in the cash book such as direct debits, interest and charges from the bank statements to keep the cash books and bank statements in balance.

Cash received should be banked regularly and intact. For example, all receipts for a particular day should be banked together. This will allow you to check amounts recorded in the cash book against amounts appearing on the bank statement.

Sales day book

If you give your customers credit, credit sales should first be entered in the sales day book and the cash only entered in the sales day book and cash book when received. You should record the date, customer's name, invoice number, total amount, VAT amount and net amount. Further columns should provide for the amount received, discounts given (if any) and date received. Copies of invoices sent to customers should be filed either by customer or number order. When the invoice is paid it should be marked as such and transferred to a permanent file. The sales day book, when totalled, will therefore record the total of the business's debtors and show the debts in order of age. This will allow you to follow up unpaid debts readily. You should keep records of telephone conversations and correspondence for all debts to help you.

Purchase day book

If you are given credit by suppliers, you should maintain a purchase day book to record all invoices received and the date paid. As invoices are paid this should be recorded in the purchase day book and cash book. For each invoice you should record the date, supplier's name, VAT element, total and net amount and date paid. If you have only a few suppliers, you can further analyse creditors by supplier; alternatively, a separate record by supplier could be maintained. Again, keep all unpaid invoices filed separately and transfer them to a permanent file when paid.

The purchase day book will total the amount outstanding to suppliers.

Petty cash book

This book should record all minor spending made from cash held in the business. To maintain control it is best to start a petty cash float rather than allow payments 'out of the till'. The float should, of course, be kept in a locked box and the amount kept at a minimum for your needs – perhaps £50.

SALES DAY BOOK

DATE	CUSTOMER	INV NO	TOTAL	VAT	FOOD SALES	BEVERAGE SALES	TOBACCO SALES	MISC SALES	DATE PAID	AMOUNT RECEIVED	DISCOUNT GIVEN
1.1	C Brown	136	223.00	33.20	104.80	85.00					
3.1	D Bassett	137	45.00	6.70	33.20	5.10					
4.1	OPQ Ltd	138	89.00	13.20	75.80						
TOTAL											

PURCHASE DAY BOOK

DATE	SUPPLIER	INV NO	TOTAL	VAT	FOOD PURCHASE	BEVERAGE PURCHASE	TOBACCO PURCHASE	MISC PURCHASE	DATE PAID	AMOUNT PAID	DISCOUNT RECEIVED
2.1	Dairies Ltd	469	22.00	3.28	18.72						
8.2	Butchers & Co	32	36.00	5.36		30.64					
9.2	P F & Co	124	66.30	9.87	56.43						
TOTAL											

QUERY – ANALYSIS OF ACCOUNTS RECEIVABLE ITEMS

Start the float by drawing the money from the bank and recording the amount in the cash book and petty cash book. Each time money is taken from the float, this should be recorded in the petty cash book and analysed by type of expenditure. You should always keep receipts and if necessary record VAT. To top up the float, summarise the receipts to ensure that they add up to the amounts in the book. Draw a cheque on the bank for this amount. There should now be the original float in the box. The cheque drawn on the bank should be analysed in the cash book according to type of expenditure.

Double entry bookkeeping

The term double entry bookkeeping frequently puts fear into the hearts of those who do not understand the phrase. Double entry bookkeeping is simply a system which ensures that the books of account described above 'balance' by recording all transactions twice – once as either expenditure on assets or costs, or income – and once as an increase or decrease in an asset or liability.

The simplified cash book above does this by recording cash received as income (analysed by type) and as an increase in the cash balance, as an asset. Cash expended is recorded as an expense (analysed by type) and as a decrease in the cash balance.

In a more complex set of accounts, a nominal or general ledger is used to record the assets and liabilities, expenditure and revenues.

Financial statements

In order to monitor your performance it is best to summarise the information in the accounting books into financial statements which can be compared against the budget for the business and performance in previous periods. Financial statements will also be useful to formulate budgets for the next period.

Financial statements should be prepared as frequently as needed for you to monitor the business. This is likely to be at least monthly. Unless you are familiar with accounting practices, it is easier to employ a bookkeeper or your accountant to draw up the financial statements from your accounting records.

As a sole trader you will be most interested in cash and profit. As a partner or director, you will also be concerned with return on investment. The three main financial statements which monitor these results are:

- Cash flow statement
- Profit and loss account
- Balance sheet

Cash flow statement

The cash flow statement summarises receipts and payments, and shows how delays in the receipt of payments affect profits before it turns into cash at the bank. The cash flow statement should be compared with the forecast for the same period to see where problems may have arisen. Using the cash flow statement to forecast further months may point out where problems could arise in the future and if there will be a need for further funding of the business.

The information for the cash flow statement will be drawn from the cash book. An example of a cash flow statement is shown on page 53. You should examine variances carefully to ensure that, where possible, corrective action is taken to improve the cash flow (and profits) of the business. This may include:

- *Better control over credit given to customers.*
  Are invoices sent out promptly?
  Is credit given on the guarantee of certain levels of business?
  Are customer references checked?
  Are discounts offered for prompt payment?
  Are credit terms such as 30 days from invoice enforced?
  Are statements sent or regular follow-ups made?
  Could you ask for deposits in advance, say, for a function?
  Could you offer alternative means of payment such as credit cards which would ensure quicker payment?
- *Better credit terms from suppliers.*
  Could you negotiate credit from cash suppliers?
  Are you taking full advantage of credit terms given?
- *Use of cash balances.*
  Are you making the best use of cash funds, minimising charges and maximising interest received?
- *Increased revenues.*
  This involves a reassessment of pricing, marketing and product suitability
- *Reduced costs.*
  Are costs right for the current level of business?
- *Stock levels.*
  Do stocks need to be kept at current levels or could they be reduced?
  Could certain items be paid for on call-off from a supplier?

Profit and loss account

The profit and loss account summarises the sales made in the period (although not necessarily paid for) against the expenditure incurred to achieve those sales (although not necessarily paid for). The difference is the profit earned or loss for the business for that period. One can see how a business may show a profit, but owing to the pattern of cash flows be showing an overdraft on the cash flow statement. A profitable business can easily find itself under threat of receivership if it is unable to pay for debts or new supplies.

The profit and loss account is summarised from the expenditure and income analysis in the cash book (or purchases and sales day books where credit is given or taken). Adjustments will need to be made to the profit and loss account to arrive at the profit to be assessed for taxation purposes.

Balance sheet

The balance sheet records the assets and liabilities of the business. Assets will include purchased capital items as well as debtors, stocks and cash balances.

CASH FLOW FORECAST FOR THE PERIOD...

	JAN £	FEB £	MARCH £	APRIL £	MAY £	JUNE £	JULY £	AUG £	SEPT £	OCT £	NOV £	DEC £
RECEIPTS (INCLUDING VAT)												
CASH SALES	2000	2500	2750	2750	2750	2000	2000	2000	2500	2750	2750	4000
CREDIT SALES	9000	7000	8500	8500	8500	6000	6000	6000	8000	8500	9000	12000
MISCELLANEOUS												
TOTAL	11000	9500	11250	11250	11250	8000	8000	8000	10500	11250	11750	16000
EXPENDITURE												
FOOD AND BEVERAGE	3520	3040	3600	3600	3600	2560	2560	2560	3360	3600	3760	5120
WAGES – NET	500	500	500	500	500	500	500	500	500	500	500	1000
PAYE AND NI	240	120	120	120	120	120	120	120	120	120	120	120
GENERAL EXPENSES	200	200	200	200	200	200	200	200	200	200	200	200
INCOME TAX					4000						3500	
VAT	3500			3058			3216			2543		
CAPITAL ITEMS				500					2000			
RENT	1500	1500	1500	1500	1500	1500	1500	1500	1500	1500	1500	1500
RATES	500	500	500	500	500	500	500	500	500	500	500	500
LIGHT AND HEAT			480			550			400			600
TELEPHONE AND POST	100	100	100	100	100	100	100	100	100	100	100	100
BANK CHARGES	50	50	50	50	50	50	50	50	50	50	50	50
BOOKKEEPER	200	200	200	200	200	200	200	200	200	200	200	200
PROFESSIONAL FEES			2500									
INSURANCE	100	100	100	100	100	100	100	100	100	100	100	100
LOAN INTEREST AND DRAWINGS		2200			2200			2200			2200	
DRAWINGS	800	800	800	800	800	800	800	800	800	800	800	800
TOTAL PAYMENTS	11210	9310	10650	11228	13870	7180	9846	8830	9830	10213	13530	10290
NET CASH FLOW FOR MONTH	-210	190	600	22	-2620	820	-1846	-830	670	1037	-1780	5710
BALANCE BROUGHT FORWARD	2200	1990	2180	2780	2802	182	1002	-844	-1674	-1004	33	-1747
CLOSING BANK BALANCE	1990	2180	2780	2802	182	1002	-844	-1674	-1004	33	-1747	3963

CASH FLOW STATEMENT FOR THE PERIOD...

	APRIL £ BUDGET	APRIL £ ACTUAL	VARIANCE	MAY £ BUDGET	JUNE £ BUDGET	JULY £ BUDGET	AUG £ BUDGET	SEPT £ BUDGET	OCT £ BUDGET	NOV £ BUDGET	DEC £ BUDGET
RECEIPTS (INCLUDING VAT)											
CASH SALES	2750	2500	−250	2750	2000	2000	2000	2500	2750	2750	4000
CREDIT SALES	8500	7950	−550	8500	6000	6000	6000	8000	8500	9000	12000
MISCELLANEOUS											
TOTAL	11250	10450	−800	11250	8000	8000	8000	10500	11250	11750	16000
EXPENDITURE											
FOOD AND BEVERAGE	3600	3250	−350	3600	2560	2560	2560	3360	3600	3760	5120
WAGES – NET	500	498	−2	500	500	500	500	500	500	500	1000
PAYE AND NI	120	120	0	120	120	120	120	120	120	120	120
GENERAL EXPENSES	200	186	−14	200	200	200	200	200	200	200	200
INCOME TAX				4000				2000		3500	
VAT	3058	2938	−120			3216			2543		
CAPITAL ITEMS	500	420	−80								
RENT	1500	1500	0	1500	1500	1500	1500	1500	1500	1500	1500
RATES	500	500	0	500	500	500	500	500	500	500	500
LIGHT AND HEAT					550			400			600
TELEPHONE AND POST	100	92	−8	100	100	100	100	100	100	100	100
BANK CHARGES	50	32	−18	50	50	50	50	50	50	50	50
BOOKKEEPER	200	200	0	200	200	200	200	200	200	200	200
PROFESSIONAL FEES											
INSURANCE	100	100	0	100	100	100	100	100	100	100	100
LOAN INTEREST AND DRAWINGS				2200			2200			2200	
DRAWINGS	800	750	−50	800	800	800	800	800	800	800	800
TOTAL PAYMENTS	11228	10586	−642	13870	7180	9846	8830	9830	10213	13530	10290
NET CASH FLOW FOR MONTH	22	−136	−158	−2620	820	−1846	−830	670	1037	−1780	5710
BALANCE BROUGHT FORWARD	2360	2360	0	2224	−396	424	−1422	−2252	−1582	−545	−2325
CLOSING BANK BALANCE	2802	2224	−578	−396	424	−1422	−2252	−1582	−545	−2325	3385

ABC CATERERS
PROFIT AND LOSS ACCOUNT FOR THE PERIOD...

	APRIL ACTUAL £	APRIL BUDGET £	VARIANCE £
REVENUE (NET)			
FOOD	8000	8500	(500)
BEVERAGE	2560	3000	(440)
MISCELLANEOUS	240	150	90
TOTAL	10800	11650	(850)
LESS COST OF SALES			
Opening stock	400	400	0
Purchases (net)	3400	3600	200
	3800	4000	200
Less Closing stock	750	650	(100)
Cost of sales	3050	3350	300
GROSS PROFIT	7750	8300	(550)
OTHER EXPENSES			
Payroll costs	618	618	0
Other expenses	279	200	(79)
Light and heat	120	160	40
Telephone and post	85	100	15
Bank charges	50	50	0
Bookkeeper	200	200	0
Professional fees			
TOTAL OTHER EXPENSES	1352	1328	(24)
FIXED EXPENSES			
Rent	1500	1500	0
Rates	500	500	0
Insurance	100	100	0
TOTAL FIXED EXPENSES	2100	2100	0
NET PROFIT	4298	4872	(574)
INCOME TAX	1075	1218	144
NET INCOME	3223	3654	(431)

AMOUNTS IN BRACKETS INDICATE A NEGATIVE VARIANCE

ABC CATERERS
BALANCE SHEET AS AT 19XX

	19XX	19XY
ASSETS		
Current assets		
Bank accout		
Cash		
Debtors		
Stocks		
Prepaid expenses		
Total current assets	_____	_____
Fixed assets		
Buildings		
Furnishings and equipment		
Operating equipment		
Vehicles		
Total	_____	_____
Less accumulated depreciation	_____	_____
Net property and equipment	_____	_____
Other assets	_____	_____
Total assets	_____	_____
LIABILITIES AND EQUITY		
Current liabilities		
Creditors		
PAYE, NI and VAT		
Accrued expenses		
Other		
Total current liabilities	_____	_____
Long-term debt		
Loans		
Total long-term debt	_____	_____
Owner's equity		
Capital		
Retained earnings	_____	_____
Total owner's equity		
Total liabilities and owner's equity	_____	_____

Liabilities will include creditors, loans and overdrafts. The balancing item is the owner's stake in the business which equates to initial owner's funds put into the business and retained profits.

Data processing systems

It is important to keep up-to-date and accurate accounting records and to compile regular financial statements. Computerisation is one way to keep records in a manageable form. There are many reasonably priced and reliable accounting programs and computers available for the small business. When investing in both the computer and printer (hardware) and various programs (software), it is advisable to seek advice. This may be from specialist consultancy firms but, for a business person wanting a small system, advice is more likely to be from other business people, local Chambers of Commerce, your Local Enterprise Agency and computer dealers.

If computers are new to you, before investing in one, it is sensible to take an evening or one-day introductory course. You will then at least learn the meaning of the terminology surrounding computers. The following are merely pointers in the complicated task of choosing a computer system:

- Decide what functions you want the computer to carry out – then define the specific tasks and the number of transactions
- Decide who will use the system and the training requirements
- Try to forecast future needs
- Visit various suppliers and discuss your requirements with them
- As well as having a demonstration, ask to 'test drive' suitable systems, preferably under similar conditions
- Check the supplier's terms and conditions of sale
- Check after-sales support and training given.

As with most things, you get what you pay for. As a first-time user, it is best to look at well-known tried and tested products. The key element in choosing the right system lies in identifying the software options which suit your specific business requirements exactly. The choice of software, in most cases, determines the choice of computer.

Computers with appropriate software can also be useful for letters, labels, invoices and keeping customer information for the preparation of mailing lists. Therefore the possibilities of using computer systems to improve the marketing of the business must not be underestimated.

Data Protection Act

Under this Act, if you maintain certain types of data such as information about individuals, your business must be registered with the Data Protection Registrar. Users of the data are required to observe rules of confidentiality and accuracy and the data subjects have rights to inspect any information about themselves.

Taxation

Deborah Griffin

The regulations governing the various forms of tax can be complicated and the penalties for late or inaccurate payment onerous. It is also easy to overpay tax by not claiming all the expenditure allowed, or incorrectly completing the various tax returns. It is therefore essential that proper accounting records are maintained. The advice of an accountant is likely to be worthwhile in both minimising the liability to tax and ensuring that the requirements of VAT and PAYE investigators are fully met.

Value Added Tax (VAT)

Each year the government sets a level of turnover, above which your business must register for VAT. Simply, you must pay over to Customs and Excise the amount of VAT collected on sales, less the VAT paid on purchases. This may be paid over monthly or quarterly and there are onerous penalties for late payment or non-registration.

Below the set level of turnover, you do not have to charge VAT on your sales, neither can you claim back VAT paid on purchases. You can register for VAT even if you are below the set level. The decision will depend on the market in which you operate. Do your customers expect to pay VAT and can they claim it back? Are most of your competitors adding VAT to sales? Some types of sales and purchases are exempt from VAT. Below a set level of turnover, you may also opt to pay VAT on a cash basis, that is when cash is received and paid, or on an accruals basis, that is when sales and purchases are incurred. Because of the complexity of the regulations, it is advisable to take advice from your accountant.

The books that you have set up should be adequate to keep records on VAT. There are complications such as VAT on imports and some business entertaining with which you will need to be familiar. You should also expect an annual visit from Customs and Excise to ensure that proper records are being maintained and the correct amounts paid over.

Customs and Excise provide a free booklet, 'Should I register for VAT?'

PAYE and National Insurance

If you choose to employ staff, PAYE and National Insurance implications arise. You should approach the Inland Revenue (each area will have its own office, usually not many miles from where you are located), who will supply all the necessary forms, guides and booklets with an Employer's Starter Pack which includes tables for operating PAYE and National Insurance payments.

Even so, it can be a complicated business and you may wish to seek advice from your accountant. This is particularly the case for catering businesses where gratuities and service charges may be collected and such 'perks' as free meals liable to assessment as benefits.

You are obliged to collect a Form P45 from each new employee and to provide a payslip detailing pay and deductions made.

The payroll records are maintained on Form P11, a deductions working sheet, for each employee. These must be retained for three years. A summary sheet (Form 14) is completed. Payment of PAYE and NI contributions is made to the Inland Revenue either monthly or, for smaller businesses, quarterly, to be received by the Revenue by the 19th of the following month.

At the end of the year summary sheets (Form P14) must be completed and a P60 provided to the employee summarising the pay and deductions for the year.

Remember, the business must pay NI on an employee's salary – it is therefore an additional cost to the business.

Where a service charge is made to guests and redistributed to staff by the employer, this forms part of taxable pay. Tips paid to the staff directly must be declared to the Inland Revenue on staff annual tax returns.

Where tips and gratuities are paid into a tronc and distributed by a troncmaster or tronc committee, the tronc master or committee is responsible for deducting PAYE from payments out of the tronc and making the appropriate returns to the Inland Revenue.

Income tax on profits and income

If you are a sole trader or in a partnership, you must still pay income tax but you have the benefit that it is payable only twice yearly based on the previous year's profits. It is essential to provide for this payment out of the business's income. Remember, if your profits are growing, you may be liable for more tax than has been assessed. Conversely, if your profits have fallen, you may be over-assessed for tax. You can appeal against an over-assessment.

Directors of a company are employers and usually pay tax as PAYE and the business must also pay the appropriate NI.

Corporation Tax

Where your business has been set up as a limited company, the profits of the company are liable to Corporation Tax. This is payable nine months after the year-end date in which the profit was made. Losses may be carried forward to set off against profits made in future years to reduce the tax liability.

Capital Gains Tax

A new business is unlikely to have to deal with this tax except when taking over a family business or other going concern. Capital Gains Tax may arise when the business or business assets are sold or a partner leaves or dies. The sole trader or partner should be aware of his or her liability for this tax by taking advice.

2.3

Billing Control

Deborah Griffin

Billing

At the end of a meal or function the customer needs to have a properly itemised bill, correctly totalled and precisely reflecting what was ordered and served and the price stated on the menu or letter of confirmation. The bill must be absolutely correct with nothing added and nothing left off. The system employed must achieve these objectives, otherwise there will be either customer dissatisfaction or a shortfall in sales. Generally speaking, the smaller the operation the simpler the system.

There are many styles of bill presentation from the simple handwritten one to the sophisticated and computerised. The chosen style and method should be appropriate to the type of business being operated. Whatever the style or system, the bill must be clear and laid out in such a way as to ensure that the customer understands it. It should be immediately obvious what each charge refers to. The system must also take into account the internal accounting methods which will probably require food sales to be separate from liquor sales and any other sundry sales if relevant to the operation.

Bills should be numbered to help identification and control. Waiting staff can then be issued with a set number of bills with consecutive numbers which, when issued, should be recorded on a bill control sheet. This ensures that bills do not go 'missing' without being noticed. If they do, the member of staff who 'lost' the bill can be identified.

Checking

Most checking systems will have two objectives. First, a copy check will be used to order food items from the chef or liquor items from the dispense bar. Second, another copy of the check should serve as a control to ensure that all ordered items have been correctly entered on a customer's bill. This is done by matching each check to the appropriate customer bill at the end of the day.

Checking systems range from a one-, two- or three-part handwritten system to a fully computerised system such as Remanco.

Credit

The decision to give your customers credit is one to be carefully considered. The granting of credit will involve additional expense through

- a delay in receiving cash and the consequences on the business cash flow
- the extra work involved in invoicing and subsequent collection of debts
- the possibility of debts becoming irrecoverable.

The decision must therefore be based on an assessment of the extra business which is likely to be encouraged by giving credit. Even the fact that a competing business gives credit may be insufficient reason if your product is preferred.

For one-off functions to private individuals it is advisable to receive most of the amount to be billed before the function begins. Once the function is over there is little incentive to settle the account. Private individuals should not as a rule be granted credit – it is easier for an individual to 'disappear' than a company.

When granting credit it is advisable to ask the customer to complete a credit application form. This should detail the following:

- Full company name and address
- Contact name and telephone number
- Name of bankers, address and account number
- Names of two other trade references with contact names and addresses
- Names and signatures of company personnel authorised to sign on behalf of the company.

The form should detail the terms and conditions of granting credit. These might include the following terms:

- Accounts to be settled in full on receipt of invoice
- In the event of accounts not being settled within 15 days 'the business' reserves the right to suspend or withdraw credit facilities

- There is a credit limit of £ x.

Bank and trade references should be followed up to ascertain the suitability of the customer for granting credit.

Once credit has been given it is important that tight control is maintained over the debtors. Each day cash taken and credit given should total the revenue for the day as recorded by a point of sale machine or manual listing of sales. Credit sales will be recorded in the sales day book.

A check should be made to ensure that invoices are sent to the value of the credit given. Invoices should be sent promptly to customers. Invoices will be recorded separately in the sales day book and copies kept in files either by customer or numerically. Where there are a large number of credit customers a separate sales ledger should be created. This will record invoices and payments by customer. A file for each customer should be created and invoices filed by customer.

It is often worthwhile telephoning the customer several days later to ensure that the invoice has been received and is correct from the customer's point of view.

On a regular basis (perhaps weekly) outstanding debts should be chased. Where there are only a few credit customers outstanding debts will most easily be seen from the sales day book where debts are recorded in chronological order. For larger sales ledgers a review of all debts should be undertaken regularly. Notes of action taken such as telephone calls, letters sent and debt collection should be recorded. Statements should be sent on a regular basis – some companies only pay when a statement is received!

Credit cards

Credit cards are another form of credit and the same considerations apply to accepting credit cards as to giving credit generally. Credit cards are a form of credit where the debtor becomes the credit card company.

For each credit card an agreement will be signed with the appropriate company. The commission charged to the business usually depends on the level of turnover likely to be processed by each credit card (usually between 1 and 4 per cent). A small catering company is likely to be charged the maximum commission. This is therefore a direct cost to be considered when deciding whether to accept credit cards.

There is also the possibility of losing money owing to credit card fraud and the additional administration involved.

The credit card companies will supply the documentation, 'swipe' machine and signage. It is important to ensure that you and your staff are well trained in the checking and completion of each credit card to avoid costly mistakes. Businesses are usually set a limit of credit to be given per transaction. Over this amount, authority must be sought from the credit card company.

For credit cards, the customer slips can be processed through the bank and payment received into the bank net of commission. Charge card slips such as American Express and Diners Card are usually submitted to the company and payment received by cheque, again net of commission.

Under the Credit Cards (Price Discrimination) Order 1990, businesses are now able to levy a surcharge to customers for payments by credit card or make an adjustment to payments in cash. Any such practice must be notified to customers either by a notice at the public entrance or at points where payment is made. This does not appear to have become common practice and your decision to charge extra must be based on assessment of the effect on customer demand and the competition.

Invoices

In most businesses you will need to provide an invoice to the customer. You can purchase duplicated invoice books from stationers. These should be consecutively numbered and the number recorded on the back of cheques and on credit card vouchers to identify payments. If you are registered for VAT, there are certain legal requirements of the 'tax invoice'. It must include:

- An identifiable and unique invoice number
- Your VAT registration number
- The business name and registered address
- The date of supply of the goods or service
- The customer's name and address
- A description of services/goods invoiced
- The charge made for each description excluding VAT
- The rate of VAT
- The total charge excluding VAT
- The total VAT payable
- The total payable
- Details of any cash discount offered.

Bank and Cash Controls

Deborah Griffin

The importance of cash to the business has been stressed. Cash means not only physical cash held but also funds in the bank account. The following controls should be adhered to in order to optimise cash and bank balances:

- The physical security of cheques and cash held in the business should be considered. This may include the installation of safes, security over keys and regular collection of cash from points of sale (see pages 219–220).
- Cheque and cash receipts should be banked regularly and cash held on the premises should be at a minimum. Cash in the hand does not earn interest.
- The trustworthiness and employment history of any employees handling cash should be verified (see pages 196–197).
- You should understand the terms of the bank accounts which the business uses to ensure that charges and interest incurred are minimised and interest received maximised.
- Maximise the interest-earning potential of your cash balance by readily transferring funds to higher interest-earning accounts.
- Each month the bank statement should be reconciled to the cash book to ensure that all entries are entered correctly.
- Interest rates on arranged overdrafts or loans are usually cheaper than unauthorised overdrafts. The cash flow forecast will enable you to predict when you might need cash.

Budgetary Control

Deborah Griffin

A successful business makes careful plans and then makes them happen. After the initial business plan has been made (see pages 13–15), it is essential to fine tune your projections as more information becomes available to you. Planning is a continuous process and, as actual results become available, the information should be used to plan for subsequent periods.

Actual results should always be compared to plans to check progress and identify areas that need attention. Three disciplines are fundamental to running businesses well – making plans, reviewing actual results and taking corrective action. In previous sections we have discussed making plans and the production of regular financial statements showing the results of the business. These financial accounts, when produced within two to three weeks of the month or quarter being reported on and compared to plans made, form the management accounts of the business.

Management, be it the sole trader, the partners or directors of a company, should investigate and understand the reasons for all major differences between actual results and plans (budgets). Management control is the process of ensuring that resources are obtained and used effectively to achieve the objectives of the business. The cycle of control is therefore as follows:

- formulate the plan
- record the plan
- carry out the plan
- monitor performance against the plan
- evaluate and control.

Effective management control means being aware of changes that threaten earnings and cash flows, and counteracting them and identifying opportunities for greater profitability.

Variance Analysis

Deborah Griffin

Variance analysis is a means of assessing performance, but it is only a method of identifying weakness where controlling action might be necessary by identifying areas for investigation. Small variances within acceptable tolerances can be ignored. Other variances may indicate excessive expenditure which is controllable or shortfalls in income which are also controllable. These should always be investigated. Examples of variances which may be controllable are:

- A price increase by a regular supplier – it may be possible to purchase goods elsewhere
- Seasonal price changes or changes in price of one product. It may be possible to change menus or presentation to reduce exposure to the price increases
- Changes in demand for particular menu items or products for sale, perhaps as a result of consumer trends, seasonality or competitor influence. Appropriate action may require a change of product offered or improvements in the product.

There may also be a need to increase the selling price of your own products. This must, of course, be considered against competitive pressures and the customer profile.

Uncontrollable variances may arise, such as with an increase in rents or rates. This will have an effect on the overall profitability of the business and care must be taken to ensure that their impact on planned earnings is minimised. Again, this may require an assessment of your selling prices or turnover.

Ratio and trend analysis

Ratio analysis is concerned with the relationship of various items in the accounts. By recording these ratios on a month-to-month basis it is possible to spot trends in the business's performance. Ratios may also be compared to planned ratio goals or industry averages where available. Like variance analysis, ratios are only indicators to financial performance. Operating ratios commonly used in the catering industry include:

- *Average food check or average spend per cover*
  This is calculated by dividing total food revenue by the number of covers. 'Covers' refers to guests served during the period.
- *Food cost percentage*
  This is calculated by dividing the cost of food sales by total food revenue (see pages 102–103).
- *Beverage cost percentage*
  This is calculated by dividing the cost of beverage sales by total beverage revenue.
- *Labour cost percentage*
  In a catering business, labour can be the largest expense. Labour costs include all payroll and related expenditure such as employer's National Insurance contributions. The labour cost percentage is calculated by dividing the total payroll and related expenditure by the total revenue. In a large concern this will be done by department.
- *Average days of stock held or stock turnover*
  Generally the lower the number of days held or the higher stock turnover, the better performance of the business. The stock turnover is calculated by dividing the cost of sales (of food or beverage) by the average stock (of food or beverage) held for the period. The number of days of stock held is calculated by dividing the number of days in the period by the stock turnover.
- *Average collection period*
  As discussed previously, the control of debtors is an important area for cash control. The average collection period is calculated by dividing the total revenue derived from credit by the average accounts receivable for the period to obtain the accounts receivable turnover. This is then divided into the number of days in the period to calculate the average collection period.
- *Profit margin*
  The profit margin ratio is calculated by dividing net income by total revenue.

Graphical representation of ratios is useful for highlighting trends or abnormal results.

Part Three

Legal Requirements

Brian Ridgway and Judy Ridgway

Almost every aspect of business is now covered by legislation. Some of this legislation will need to be taken into account at the planning and preparatory stages. The premises, for example, will need to be checked out in the light of the Fire Precautions Act, the Food Act, and the Offices, Shops and Railway Premises Act among others. The rest will come into play when you apply for a licence, employ staff and open the doors of your establishment.

Much of the legislation is extremely complicated and you may need to take expert advice. However, some government and local government departments issue booklets explaining what the requirements are and how they are likely to affect your business. A number of Acts are published with detailed Codes of Practice and copies can be obtained from HMSO headquarters and HMSO bookshops.

The Caterer and Hotelkeeper publishes a 'Guide to the Law' for hotel and catering managers which is invaluable and the Hotel Catering and Institutional Management Association also publishes useful technical fact sheets.

The Premises

Brian Ridgway and Judy Ridgway

Planning permission for your business should be sought from the local authority before you rent or buy the property. This should not be too difficult to acquire if the premises are already being used for some kind of catering. In any event, the Planning Committee will want to see detailed proposals including plans for any structural alterations. If there is a change of use involved you may have to go into much more detail, including how the new business will affect the immediate neighbourhood.

It makes sense to check your plans out with your local Fire Officer and Environmental Health Officer before completing your proposal. They may be able to point out errors and omissions which could hold up approval.

Here is a checklist of the relevant legislation and codes of practice which could affect the plans for your premises.

Electricity at Work Regulations 1989
Key points. The regulations are concerned with electrical systems, equipment and appliances which must all be soundly constructed and maintained so as to pose no danger when properly used. Only qualified personnel should be allowed to use such equipment.

Practical implications. Managers should know the location, state of repair and maintenance record of every item of electrical equipment on their premises and they should set up a regular inspection and maintenance programme. Employees using any electrical equipment of any kind should receive training to do so safely.

Fire Precautions Act 1971
Key points. A fire certificate may be compulsory under either the Fire Precautions (Hotels and Boarding Houses) Order 1972 or the Fire Precautions (Factories, Offices, Shops and Railway Premises) Order 1976.

Practical implications. Very small businesses may not be affected but it is still sensible to have any premises checked by your local Fire Officer as all companies are bound by the Act. The Act also covers fire precaution systems, fire prevention, fire fighting, fire training, testing equipment and logging findings, and means of escape. Instructions and drills will vary according to the layout and size of the premises. They should be discussed and agreed with the Fire Officer.

Food and Drugs (Control of Premises Act 1976) and Food Safety Act 1990

Key points. These are mainly enabling Acts but they need to be studied if premises are to be newly converted. They also cover the requirements for delivery vehicles.

Food Hygiene Regulations

Key points. These cover the suitability of construction and decoration of the premises as well as systems such as lighting, ventilation, water and waste (see Sections 1 and 7).

Food Premises (Registration) Regulations

Key points. Catering premises must be registered with the local Department of Environmental Health. Applications for registration must be made at least 28 days before opening.

Health and Safety at Work Act 1974

Key points. Some aspects of the Act may affect conversion work (see Section 3.5, page 77).

Occupiers Liability Act 1957 and 1984

Key points. This Act regulates the common duty of care which an occupier of premises has towards his visitors.

Practical implications. Managers must ensure that visitors will be reasonably safe when on their premises and they would be well advised to take out public liability insurance in addition to the compulsory insurance required by law. It should also be noted that, under the Unfair Contract Terms Act 1977, posting a notice that visitors use the premises at their own risk will not enable the manager to avoid liability if negligence is proved.

Offices, Shops and Railway Premises Act 1963

Key points. Deals with, among other items, the provision of clean working premises with sufficient lighting, heating, working space and sanitation. It also deals with the safety of the premises, the machinery and first aid.

Practical implications. Managers must set out rules and regulations on the installation and maintenance of lifts and machinery. They must also provide first aid boxes for every 150 employees and report accidents to the local authority. The provisions of the Health and Safety (First Aid) Regulations 1981 also apply.

Public Health (Recurring Nuisances) Act 1969
Key points. Statutory nuisances include excessive refuse, occurrence of loud and unnecessary noise, strong odours and the like.

3.2

The Food

Brian Ridgway and Judy Ridgway

The Food Safety Act and its attendant Food Hygiene Regulations 1990 are the most important and far-reaching pieces of legislation in this area and managers will need to be familiar with all their aspects.

One of the provisions of the Food Safety Act 1990 is the principle of due diligence. If a company can show that it has taken all reasonable precautions and exercised 'due diligence' to avoid an offence under the Act it can greatly reduce the possibility of prosecution.

In practice this means the setting up of control systems for all aspects of food preparation, production and service. This includes the cleanliness of the premises and machinery. It also includes assurances from suppliers that they too have taken due care. Such control systems must be regularly checked and recorded, often by means of a log book, to see that they are operating properly and staff must be trained to implement them correctly.

Legislation dealing with the use of preservatives, minimum contents levels for certain ingredients and labelling can also be important for certain types of operation, particularly if you are running a freezer service or supplying a shop. Claims made about produce must be within the Trade Descriptions Act and a working knowledge of the Weights and Measures Act is useful.

Here is a checklist of the legislation concerning the food side of the business.

Food Act 1984

This Act brings together all the previous law on the subject and establishes a system whereby the consumer is protected against inferior products and ministerial control is exercised over the preparation and service of food and its contents. It replaces the Food and Drugs Act 1955 and the Food and Drug Act Scotland 1956.

Provisions of Act

The Act makes it a grievous offence to sell, offer or expose for sale, or have in possession:

a)   that which is intended for human consumption but is unfit for human consumption. It is also an offence to deliver such food;

b)   food and drink which is not of the nature, substance or quality demanded.

Food Safety Act 1990

Key points. This is mainly an enabling Act and many of the technical details and rules governing the preparation and storage, presentation and sale of food are contained in specific food handling and hygiene regulations (see below). The Act echoes the provisions of the Food Act in making it an offence to sell food which is in any way harmful to the recipients or which is falsely labelled or which is not of the quality demanded, ie food which is not of the nature, quality or substance demanded by the purchaser.

Food Hygiene Regulations 1970 amended 1990 and Food Hygiene (Scotland) Regulations 1959

Key points. All food handlers must undergo food hygiene training on courses run either by the food authorities or by an accredited training department. The regulations lay down rules for personal hygiene and clothing and for the provision of sanitary conveniences and washhand basins for staff.

The regulations also cover the cleanliness of premises and the suitability of their construction and decoration, cleanliness of articles and equipment including lighting and ventilation, water systems and facilities for washing food and equipment, the sale and delivery of open food, the avoidance of contamination of all kinds and the reporting of any cases of food poisoning in any staff or customers.

The regulations lay down strict temperature controls for certain foods, giving maximum temperatures at which different foods should be stored.

Practical implications. These are many and varied and managers are advised to study the regulations in some detail.

Food Hygiene Market Stalls and Delivery Vehicles 1966

Key points. Standards are set for goods delivery vehicles.

Food Premises (Registration) Regulations

Key points. Every food business must be registered with its local Environmental

Health Department. Applications for registration must be made at least 28 days before opening.

Food Labelling Act 1984 amended by the Food Labelling (Amendments) Regulations 1989 and Food Labelling (Amendment Irradiated Food) 1990

Key points. This deals with all aspects of labelling and indications of ingredients and prohibits items on the premises after the 'use by' date.

Prevention of Damage by Pests Act 1959 and Public Health Act 1936 amended 1961

Key points. This deals with all aspects of pest control and the cleanliness of the premises, the drains and vermin.

Trade Descriptions Act 1968

Key points. This deals with the way in which produce, services or facilities are described and sold.

Practical implications. Care must be taken in this connection with all claims made on brochures, tariff sheets, menus, wine lists, leaflets, advertisements and signs, to avoid false or misleading statements, including false indications of origin.

Weights and Measures Act 1963 amended 1979

Key points. This Act is particularly important to caterers selling pre-packed produce.

The Drinks

Brian Ridgway and Judy Ridgway

Obtaining a licence to sell alcoholic drinks can sometimes be as much of a headache as getting planning permission. Of course, outside caterers do not generally need a licence but they need an occasional licence if they are catering to the public at a county show or a race meeting. However, the licence will only be granted to an existing licensee or eligible organisation or club. Licences are not usually needed for private parties. A useful book is the *ABC of Licensing Law* published by the National Licensed Victuallers Association.

Getting a full licence can involve a great deal of work. You will have to provide full details of the premises with structural details, plans and layout. You must provide personal details to show that you are a fit and proper person to hold a licence, as well as evidence that the premises have been properly inspected by the local authority and the business registered as necessary. You may even have to show that there is a real need for your business in the area as you may have to fight off objections from other traders.

Thought will need to be given to the type of licence required and once it is obtained you will have to apply regularly for renewal. This is not automatic. The choice of licence includes a restaurant licence where alcoholic drinks can only be served to those who are eating a table meal, a wine only or beer and wine licence or a full on-licence (see pages 31–32).

Here is a checklist of legislation covering this.

Licensing Act 1964 and 1988 and the Licensing (Scotland) Act 1976

Key points. All aspects of licences, permitted hours and the sale and consumption of alcoholic liquor are covered.

Practical implications. If you plan to sell alcohol it is important that you apply for a licence in your own right well before opening and that you familiarise yourself with the contents of the Act.

Licensing (Low Alcohol Drinks) Act 1990
Key points. This act allows drinks containing less than 0.5 per cent alcohol to be sold freely.

Food Labelling Act 1984 amended by the Food Labelling (Amendment) Regulations 1989
Key points. The provision of information on the size and strength of alcoholic drinks is covered.

Weights and Measures Act 1963 amended 1979 and Weights and Measures (Intoxicating Liquor) Order 1988
Key points. These prescribe the quantity in which certain types of alcoholic drinks must be served.

Alcoholic Liquor Duties Act 1970
Key points. Under this Act it is an offence to sell proprietary spirits which are diluted.

Children and Young Persons Act 1992
Cigarettes or tobacco. This Act prohibits the sale of cigarettes or tobacco to young persons under the age of 16, which includes vending machines; and a warning statement of an agreed size must be at the point of sale.

The Music

Brian Ridgway and Judy Ridgway

If you are running a hotel or restaurant you may well decide that some music or dancing is appropriate. If so you will need to be familiar with the relevant legislation. Outside caterers, too, should be aware of its existence in case they are booking or working with live musicians. Here is a checklist.

Copyright, Designs and Patents Act 1988
Key points. This covers the need to obtain the permission of the copyright holder to play any piece of music which is in copyright. Copyright extends from the moment the piece was composed plus 50 years after the composer's death.

Practical implications. The Performing Right Society represents the interests of individual copyright holders and grants a 'blanket' licence for an annual fee. Manufacturers and producers of sound recordings also have separate copyright on these recordings. These companies' rights are represented by Phonographic Performance Ltd which also issues licences to make public use of sound recordings. These licences cover piped music as well as live performances.

Local Government (Miscellaneous Provisions) Act 1992, Home Counties (Music and Dancing) Licensing Act 1926, London Government Act 1963 and the Public Health Act 1936 and 1961 amended 1990 plus any local bylaws
Key points. Between them these cover the need for a music and dancing licence.

Control of Pollution Act 1974
Key points. This Act deals with the question of unnecessary noise.

Personnel: Health and Safety

Brian Ridgway and Judy Ridgway

There is a considerable body of legislation which is concerned with the safety and welfare of employees. Most of it is relevant regardless of how many you employ or whether they are full or part time. Here is a checklist.

Health and Safety at Work Act 1974

Key points. Every employer has a duty to ensure, as far as is reasonably practicable, the health, safety and welfare of all employees. The Act covers the provision of safe, well-maintained machinery and equipment; information and instructions on health and safety measures, including a written statement on general policy; and safe access to a safe and healthy work environment. The employer also has a responsibility to ensure that visiting contractors operate within the Act while on the premises.

Practical implications. Accident records should be kept and a policy statement written by the owner of the company and distributed to all employees. Safety representatives must be appointed and a safety committee formed which should sit regularly to discuss all matters of safety.

Six new health and safety laws which came into effect in 1993 put flesh on the bones of the rather general obligations contained in the Act by superimposing more specific obligations.

Health and Safety (Display Screen Equipment) Regulations 1992

These regulations apply to employees who use VDU screens regularly for lengthy periods. Typically, this includes word processor operators and data input clerks. An assessment has to be made regarding the risks involved concerning eye strain, headaches etc.

The Management of Health and Safety at Work Regulations 1992

The Health and Safety at Work Act left management with little or no guidance about how to organise and structure good health and safety management. The regulations specify that management must:

- carry out an assessment of all health and safety risks
- decide what arrangements are appropriate to deal with identified risks
- draw up a document detailing the findings of the assessment and the solutions
- appoint at least one person (known as the competent person) who has the training and knowledge to assist the employee to carry out all his health and safety duties
- establish emergency and evacuation procedures for dealing with imminent danger such as fire and bomb threats.

Manual Handling Operations Regulations 1992

These regulations apply to any type of manual handling operations which means not only lifting and carrying but also pushing and pulling. The Manual Handling Regulations repeat all the old laws which had emphasis on weight alone and they introduce the New Code which looks at body movement, the grip, confined spaces and uneven floors.

Personal Protective Equipment at Work (PPE) Regulations 1992

If personal protective equipment is necessary following the assessment carried out under the Management of Health and Safety at Work Regulations, the employer must have regard to health and safety factors in selecting such equipment, must instruct and train staff to use such equipment, and must maintain that equipment in efficient working order.

The Provision and Use of Work Equipment Regulations 1992

Existing equipment in the workplace must comply with the Equipment Safety Standards by the end of January 1996, but all new equipment bought after 1 January 1993 must comply with any EC directive relating to that equipment, so it must have an EC mark and an EC Declaration of Conformity. The regulations set out a whole catalogue of equipment safety standards.

The Workplace (Health, Safety and Welfare) Regulations 1992

These regulations cover a wide range of basic workplace safety moves and update and repeat most of the older laws. Large parts of the Offices, Shops and Railway Premises Act 1963 will be phased out and incorporated into these new regulations. The regulations cover the following aspects:

- *Health*
  Ventilation, temperature, lighting, cleanliness, waste materials, dimensions and space, work station and seating.
- *Safety*
  Maintenance of workplace equipment, conditions of floors, falling objects,

windows and transparent doors, opening and cleaning of windows, skylights, doors, gates and escalators.

* *Welfare*
Sanitary conveniences, washing facilities, drinking water, storage for clothing, changing facilities and facilities for rest and eating meals.

Health and Safety (First Aid) Regulations 1981 amended 1990

Key points. Employers must provide adequate and appropriate first aid equipment and facilities for employees (though not necessarily for guests).

Practical implications. The regulations set out in detail what constitutes adequate and appropriate facilities for the type of business and the number of employees, as well as guidelines on the contents of a first aid box and the number of qualified first aiders required.

Health and Safety (Training for Employment) Regulations 1990

Key points. Managers have a duty to provide all employees with sufficient training to ensure that they can carry out their duties safely and efficiently.

Offices, Shops and Railway Premises Act 1963

Key point. This Act does not apply to small family-run businesses where only the immediate family are employed. All premises within the Act are required to be kept in a clean state and free from obstruction. Washing and sanitary facilities and sitting areas must be supplied for staff.

Prescribed Dangerous Machines Order 1964

Key points. This deals with dangerous equipment such as chopping, mixing and slicing machines.

The Reporting of Injuries, Diseases and Dangerous Occurrences Regulations 1985

Key points. The regulations deal with four types of incident: fatal accidents, major injuries, dangerous occurrences and other accidents.

Personnel: Employment

Brian Ridgway and Judy Ridgway

As soon as you start to employ people, even if it is only yourself and even if the staff are part time, you will be liable for organising income tax deductions under the PAYE scheme and for dealing with National Insurance contributions. There is also another large body of legislation covering subjects as diverse as discrimination by sex and race, time off for public duties, and the way in which you should go about both employment and dismissal.

A checklist of the relevant legislation and Codes of Practice is set out below.

The Advisory Conciliation and Arbitration Code of Practice
Key points. This covers disciplinary practice and procedures, disclosure of information to trade unions for collective bargaining purposes, and time off for trade union duties and activities.

Disabled Persons Act 1944 and 1958
Key points. This requires all employers of more than 20 people to give employment to registered disabled personnel to a quota of 3 per cent of total staff.

Employees Statutory Sick Pay (General) Regulations 1982 amended 1991
Key points. These outline the employer's duty to pay sick pay, the length of time for which it must be paid and all attendant details.

Employers Liability (Compulsory) Insurance Act 1969
Key points. Employers must insure against any civil liability for injuries or disease sustained by employees in the course of their work and display an up-to-date certificate of insurance.

Employment Acts 1975, 1980, 1982, 1988, 1989 and 1990
Key points. These are the enabling Acts for much of the employment legislation.

Employment Protection (Consolidation) Act 1978 amended 1988 and Transfer of Undertakings 1991

Key points. This deals with all aspects of dismissal and may be particularly relevant if you are taking over a going concern. It also covers terms of contract, maternity rights, redundancy, time off for trade union or public duty, itemised wage statements, accountability and sick pay.

Equal Pay Act 1970 amended 1983

Key points. The purpose of the Act is to prevent discrimination between men and women with regard to terms and conditions of employment.

Practical implications. This Act not only covers equal pay but also equal treatment on holiday and sickness benefits, pension schemes and the like. The Act also sets out criteria for 'like work' and 'work of equal value'.

Manual Handling Operations Regulations 1992

Key points. The Act deals with the manual handling of loads such as beer kegs, heavy kitchen equipment, cartons, sacks, filing cabinets and ladders.

Practical implications. Managers must identify all those jobs which might require employees to lift heavy loads. They must see if such tasks can be avoided and, if not, must assess the risks of injury and take steps to reduce that risk through training.

National Insurance Acts 1946–1971

They deal with statutory requirements for National Insurance.

Race Relations Act 1976

Key points. The Act set up the Commission for Racial Equality and includes a Code of Practice for the elimination of racial discrimination and the promotion of equal opportunity in employment. The Act covers both direct and indirect discrimination.

Sex Discrimination Act 1975 and Equal Pay Act 1986

Key points. The Act established the Equal Opportunities Commission and includes a Code of Practice for the elimination of discrimination against anyone of either sex and the promotion of equal opportunities in employment including pay.

Shops Act 1950

Key points. This contains a variety of employment-related subjects such as meal breaks, overtime, overcrowding and trade union membership, days off for the catering trade scheme, annual holidays, Sunday working and maximum hours of work per week.

Social Security Acts 1975, 1986 and 1988 and the (Claims and Payments) Regulations 1979 amended 1982

Key points. These Acts deal with Sick Pay and all Social Security matters.

Time Off for Public Duties Order 1990

Key points. This covers the provision of time off for jury service etc.

Trade Union Reform and Employment Rights Act 1993

Key points: This Act deals with enhanced employment protection rights and the abolition of Wages Councils.

Wages Act 1986

Key points. This covers the method of payment and deductions, itemised wage statements, the payment of tax and National Insurance, the provision to be made for bank holidays, unauthorised deduction from wages, and sick pay.

Written Particulars of Employment Act 1989

Key points. Employers must provide their employees with a written statement of their terms of employment. The Act sets out details of the particulars which must be included in the statement.

Practical implications. This statement is not, as is often supposed, a contract of employment and withholding of it does not deprive an employee of his contractual rights.

Redundancy Payment Act 1965

This spells out an employer's duty of care at common law to the employee, regardless of whether the law in any of the other Acts has been broken.

Employer Liability (Defective Equipment) Act 1969

Key points. This Act deals with liability, for whatever reason, which is the employer's.

The Business

Brian Ridgway and Judy Ridgway

Companies Acts 1985 and 1989

Business Names Act 1985

Insolvency Act 1986
Key points. The law relating to companies is regulated by these Acts and relates to the type of company, the duties, appointment and disqualification of directors, the Articles and Memorandum of Association, registration, accounts and records, business names and insolvency.

Control of Substances Hazardous to Health Regulations 1988
These regulations are part of the health and safety at work legislation and require employers to take notice of substances which may cause injury or illness to employees. Employers must provide adequate protection to employees, and bring the hazard to their attention.

Data Protection Act
Key points. If you maintain a data bank with customer information you are required to register with the Data Protection Registrar and are bound by the provisions of the Act.

Gaming Act £1968 and the Amendments and Regulations made under this Act
Deals with aspects of gaming in public premises.

Hotel Proprietors' Act 1956
Key points. This covers the provision of services for, and the safety of, guests.

The Price Marking (Food and Drink on Premises) Order 1979

The order requires prices to be displayed on any premises where food and/or drink is sold for consumption there. Where food and drink is brought to the customer, for instance, in restaurants, prices must be displayed outside or near the entrance so that prospective customers can see them before entering.

Sale of Goods Act 1979

This Act deals with the implied term of contract between a buyer and a seller. Where there is a contract for the sale of goods by description, there is an implied condition that the goods will correspond with that description and are of merchantable quality.

Cancellations or no show. Having entered a contract by accepting a reservation the caterer, following cancellation or no show, may only recover damages for what he has lost, ie he may well have only lost the profit as he may not have bought the goods; for example, unopened wine – profit only; opened wine – full selling price; uncooked food – profit only unless it has a short shelf life; cooked food – full selling price.

Unfair Contract Terms Act 1977

Key points. This Act limits the effect of exclusion clauses in contracts to customers and other businesses, and prevents certain clauses having any effect whatsoever.

Late Night Refreshment Houses Act 1969 (not Scotland)

Late night catering establishments. This Act is relevant to places of refreshment which are open between 10.00pm and 5.00am and which have no liquor licence.

Supply of Goods and Services Act 1982

Key points. In a contract for the supply of a service when the supplier is acting in the course of a business, there is an implied term that the supplier will carry out the service with reasonable care and skill.

The Price Indications (Method of Payment) Regulations 1991

These regulations require traders who charge different prices for different methods of payment (such as an additional charge for payment by credit card rather than cash) to make this clear to consumers, generally through the display of notices.

Consumer Protection Act 1987

Key points. The main purposes of this Act are as follows:

1. To provide customers with a strict liability remedy against a business whose defective products cause personal injury or damage to property.
2. To deal with the supply of goods which contravene safety standards.
3. It replaces Section 11 of the Trade Descriptions Act 1968 which relates to a business that gives the consumer a misleading pricing indication or fails to correct a price indication which has become misleading for one reason or another.

Theft Act 1978

Customers who knowingly make off without paying are guilty of the offence but they must have been deliberately dishonest and known that payment was required on the spot. The customer must have 'made off' and left the premises.

Part Four

Line Management

Brian Ridgway

Once the business has been set up, the general or line manager is concerned with the efficient and profitable running of the business on a day-to-day basis. He or she is the decision-maker and the motivator, and without him or her specialist services would have no place.

The job takes in menu planning; costing and pricing; purchasing; cost and stock control; operating manuals; kitchen, service and food transport systems, and hygiene. Investigation, problem-solving and overall reviews also come within his remit. In fact, he is in charge of food and liquor control from planning and purchasing to cash received at point of sale.

In a small catering company or restaurant the owner/manager may be the finance director, sales and marketing director, and personnel director as well as the general manager. In larger organisations these specialist functions will be carried out by others but they will still report to and be dependent on decisions made by the line manager for he is the power-house of the business.

Planning the Menu

Brian Ridgway

The detail of the business starts with the planning of the menu. Whether you are running a restaurant, a banqueting suite or an outside catering company the menu is your showcase. If you are starting from scratch it will also be the mainstay of your business proposals.

Menu planning starts from your vision of the business (see pages 13–15). However, there are likely to be a number of factors which may force you to modify your ideas. So the basic question of what is to be sold and at what price will depend not only on your initial ideas but also on a realistic assessment of the information obtained from market research. Look at the average spend which can be expected from potential customers and check out the competition to see exactly what they are doing and how successful they are. (See page 24.)

The ideal menu

A good menu, at whatever price, should include a range of different fare. It needs to have a balance of ingredients, textures and colours as well as a choice of different types of cooking. Careful attention must also be paid to garnish and presentation.

Within this context decisions will need to be made on the balance of familiar (and therefore reassuring) dishes and original (and therefore exciting) dishes. Would it be sensible to include local specialities or to stick to a particular theme such as Mediterranean cuisine?

It is particularly important for an outside catering company to ensure that it has menus which are appropriate to all the occasions for which it might be catering. Menus for business catering will be different from those for buffet parties and weddings. Thought must also be given to the problems of finger food, canapés and stand-up buffets as well as sit-down meals.

Some choices will need to be made fairly early on in the decision-making process.

Restaurants

- Will there be an à la carte menu or a *prix fixe* menu or both?
- Will the same menus be available at lunch and dinner?
- Will there be an extensive choice of dishes or a small selection of high quality and imaginative dishes?
- Will there be any difference between weekdays and weekends?
- Will there be any vegetarian alternatives?

Banqueting and outside catering

- Will there be flexible menus for individual needs as well as fixed menus?
- Do the menus cover all likely requests including picnic hampers, children's parties and special diet food?

When making these decisions it is worth remembering that recent years have seen the decline of the three-course meal. This is particularly apparent at lunchtime when increased business pressures and general health consciousness have led to lighter meals with only one or two courses.

The style of service is also very relevant to the menu. Is it to be old-style silver service or will the food be plated in the kitchen? Banqueting departments and outside catering companies may use 'family service' where food is offered by the waitress for self-service or buffets.

The ideal menu must also be planned in such a way as to make use of all capacity and to even out the workload in the kitchen and service areas (see pages 132–133).

Limiting factors

There may be a number of limiting factors which will need to be taken into account before plans are finalised. These will depend upon the size of the operation and the level of business that can be expected. They include:

- The size of the kitchen and the service area.
- Is the kitchen on a different floor from the restaurant?
- The amount of storage space.
- The availability of both basic and specialised produce and the availability of regular deliveries.
- Is there likely to be expensive waste and if so can these items be used up in the next day's dishes, perhaps on the fixed menu?

Remember, too, that the more complicated and comprehensive the menus are, the more expensive the ingredients and the equipment required. The required storage space will also be greater. Chefs will need to be more highly trained and this will put up the wages bill. It may also make it difficult to replace the chefs. All this increases the amount of profit you will have to make to cover your costs.

Initial testing

Once a menu has been drawn up portion sizes must be considered and tested out. These will depend upon the menu and type of customer. For example, portions are often smaller on a fixed price menu than on an à la carte menu. Customer expectation demands larger portions in the North of England compared to the South and in working-class as against white-collar areas. Outside caterers must take into account the differences between standing buffets, self-service and waitress service.

The next step is to draw up standard recipes and set down the quality and quantity of the ingredients. This should be done for *all* the dishes that will or might be used for the foreseeable future.

Each recipe must be tested to ensure that it works and that it tastes as expected. The portions and presentations must also be checked to see that they conform to the required standard.

Once this has been done the cost can be checked (see pages 98–107) to see that it has not exceeded the required limits. If it has, there may need to be a compromise so that the dish becomes economically viable but still looks and tastes good. There is no point in offering a dish which looks good value but doesn't taste good. Equally a dish which tastes well but looks poor could still disappoint the customer.

As a final check talk to the suppliers to get an idea of price fluctuations and availability over the intended period of the menu.

Changing the menu

Once the business is up and running thought must be given to changing the menu! No business can afford to stand still and menu appraisal must go on all the time.

Here are some of the factors which need to be taken into account when deciding how frequently to change the menu.

- Can the kitchen cope with rapid changes or should change be more gradual?
- Will customers get bored if the menu is not changed regularly (kitchen and waiting staff can get bored too) or will customers be upset if their favourite dishes are removed?
- Will it be possible to change menus in such a way that customers hardly notice by removing dishes which are not selling and replacing them with new dishes suggested and developed by kitchen staff?
- Will the menu have to be reprinted for every change or is it wholly or partially handwritten?
- Will seasonal availability of ingredients necessitate a quarterly change of menu or could the menu be changed bi-annually with regular augmentation with dishes made from produce available within a limited season?

Planning the Wine List

Brian Ridgway

Here again time taken in checking the market research before planning the wine list is time well spent. If you get the wine list right the same philosophy will dictate the choice of both replacement wines and new additions.

Points to consider are:

- How much storage space do you have for wine? Remember that even if you stock a small number of bottles of each wine a large list will mean that there will be quite a large number of bottles to store and a greater amount of capital tied up in stock.
- The amount of additional money customers are likely to be prepared to spend on wine after paying for the meal.
- How sophisticated are customer wine tastes likely to be?
- What ratio of familiar to unfamiliar wines should there be? On the whole customers are not adventurous in their choices of wine.
- Do you plan to include one or more 'house wines' and will these be available by the glass?

The latter could be the most important decision to make as at least 50 per cent of your customers will go for the house wine or for the half dozen least expensive wines on the list. Some restaurants successfully offer a choice of wines by the glass from different areas and at different price levels.

A wine list should include the following elements:

Sparkling white wines. Special events call for something a little different and champagne and sparkling wines do well for business parties and private anniversaries. The Grande Marque champagnes should be represented along with a more reasonable buy. High spend restaurants might add a vintage champagne. All restaurants should also add one or two of the many sparkling wines from areas like the Loire (Saumur), Burgundy (Cremant de Bourgogne), Spain (Cava),

Germany (Sekt) or Italy (sweet and dry). Sparkling wines from Australia, New Zealand and California also offer good value for money with added interest. Some of them, like Maison Deutz and Green Point, are actually made by the French champagne houses.

Dry white wines. These take up the lion's share of the white section of the list and should include popular Chardonnay and Sauvignon Blanc based wines as well as some more adventurous choices.

Medium dry white wines. Despite the trend towards drier wines, these wines are still the most popular in the UK. Mid-European wines in this category are beginning to challenge the well-entrenched German whites. Try out wines from Hungary, Bulgaria and Austria. They are doing well in the supermarkets and could do well on your list.

Sweet white wines. These are essentially dessert or pudding wines and many restaurants make a feature of them by listing them on the back of the dessert or pudding menu or on a separate list with other after-dinner drinks such as Cognac, Armagnac and the newly popular Calvados.

Light red wines. These wines are becoming increasingly popular with the move away from drinks with high levels of alcohol. They also have very fruity flavours which modern wine drinkers find attractive.

Medium and full-bodied red wines. These are the traditional wines to serve with food. They are often based on the universal Cabernet Sauvignon but other grape varieties should also be represented.

Rosé wines. Many restaurants do not bother with rosé wines but some customers like them, particularly during the summer, so try them out as a summer offer.

Wines in all these styles are on offer from most of the wine-growing areas of the world and the choice will depend upon the theme of the restaurant and upon an assessment of the likes and dislikes of prospective customers. French and possibly German wines are the traditional choice but it is well worth considering wines from other European areas such as Bulgaria, Italy or Spain. New World wines have also become popular and are excellent value for money. Australia, New Zealand, Chile and the United States all offer very good wines.

It is quite difficult to ensure value for money at the lower end of the price scale, but customers are more likely to buy wine more regularly if it is not too expensive. There tends to be a threshold somewhere around the £8–£9 mark over which many customers will not usually go. The actual level varies in different areas and with different socio-economic groups.

In a few areas there will be a demand for fine wines. These may form part of your regular list or you could fill the demand by buying bin ends or at auction and offering fine wines as available. Here again New World wines from producers like Robert Mondavi in California and Penfolds in Australia can offer fine wines to rival those of France.

All this needs to be balanced against the price you will have to pay for the wine and the sort of cash profit you can expect (see pages 94–107). Often the expenditure of a little more money will yield a disproportionately better wine. The lower cash profit margin will be offset by the greater sales and your customers will have more confidence in your reasonably priced wines. Indeed, care shown at the cheaper end of the list is rightly taken to be indicative of the attitude taken throughout the list.

4.3

Costing and Pricing

Brian Ridgway

There is some controversy over the need to cost a menu in order to decide on the selling price. There are entrepreneurs who say that they have a feel for the right price of a dish, based on the cost of the main ingredient. A proprietor/chef who does not cook to a recipe and is continually changing dishes, perhaps on a daily basis, may have to decide on prices in this way. Otherwise too much time would be spent on the calculations.

Even so it is only prudent to cost dishes from time to time. Indeed, the purist will argue that it is important to know the likely profit of each dish on the menu.

Detailed costing enables the line manager to:

- Establish the achievable profit for each item on the menu or wine list.
- Establish precise ingredients and portion sizes.
- Discover how increases (or decreases) in food costs are affecting the profit made on each dish.
- Avoid the inclusion of loss-making dishes.

- Ensure that the costs of supporting ingredients are not forgotten. These can sometimes be quite significant and, if not fully quantified, can be a drain on profits. This is particularly so if the dish is a top seller.

Costing dishes

Start costing by drawing up a list of all the ingredients required using agreed standard recipes (see pages 98–99). Every single ingredient, however small, must be included. This means small quantities of cooking oil as well as a dash of *demi-glace* or some tomato *concassé*. It also means the garnish which is often forgotten.

Take an average price for all variable price ingredients. This avoids the problem of under-costing a dish when the main ingredient is at its lowest price. Indeed, the whole question of the seasonal variation in the cost of ingredients is particularly important to a small catering company which is not likely to change its menus.

Extra care is always needed when costing for outside catering or for banqueting facilities. Prices may be calculated and the selling price agreed with the customer some months before the event. Once the contract is signed it is not usually possible to change the menu or the price and this could result in the loss of potential profit. So build in contingency arrangements to deal with emergencies.

Ingredients, such as whole fish, cuts of meat, sprouts and cooking apples, which have to be trimmed or those where there is a loss of weight in cooking should be costed on the basis of the weight served. Costings will be inaccurate if the bought weight price is used.

Yield tests are a useful way of evaluating the true value/cost of commodities used – especially with carcase meat, fish on the bone, fresh vegetables and any high cost item.

Standard Yields

The definition of a standard yield is: an expected output from a given input. Standard yields are used so that the value of an item may be correctly assessed at its various stages of preparation.

Example:

POTATOES

Standard buying price	=	15p per lb
Yield after peeling 100lb	=	83 per cent
Yield after turning into chips	=	72 per cent

Therefore:

100lb potatoes @ 15p per lb	=	£15.00
83lb potatoes peeled value still	=	£15.00
Therefore the price per lb	=	18.07p

This in turn produces:

72lb chips value still	=	£15.00
Therefore price per lb	=	20.83p

Yields can also be used as a guide to quality for the buyer. If the quality is below standard, wastage is greater, therefore the yield is less than standard.

Here is an example of a yield test for a whole fillet of beef.

Yield Test Card

Item: Fillet of beef	lb/oz	Price per lb	Total value
Weight on delivery	5.14	£6.08	£35.72
Minus unusable fat/bone/ waste	.10		No value
Re-usable trimmings	1.60	£1.17	£1.61
Net yield usable	3.14	£8.80	£34.11

1. If a complete fillet weighs 5lb 14oz which costs £35.72 = £6.08 per lb.
2. Unusable kitchen trimming weighs 10oz – no value – pure waste.
3. Then the semi-trimmed weight is 5lb 4oz which still costs £35.72 = £6.80 per lb.
4. Reusable kitchen trimmings weigh 1lb 6oz, which when minced can be used for another dish such as lasagne. But while its true value is £9.35, the production value is £1.61 for 1lb 6oz (based on £1.17 per lb for mince). If lasagne was the only meat dish, mince would be bought at £1.17 per lb – not fillet steak at £6.08 per lb.
5. Net yield of usable meat is now 3lb 14oz which still costs £35.72, which makes the price £9.22 per lb.
6. But £1.61 was saved for another dish, so this amount is deducted from the original cost of £35.72 less £1.61 = £34.11.
7. This now means that the trimmed fillet yields 3lb 14oz, costs £34.11 which is equal to £8.80 per lb kitchen trimmed, the actual cost of the fillet ready to use.

Average Yields for Trimmed and Cooked Food Items

	Yield %
French trimmed cutlets from best ends of lamb ex market	59
Noisettes of lamb from best ends of lamb ex market	49
Trimmed steak meat from stripped loin ex market	82
Fillets of sole from whole sole ex market	51
Foreribs of beef cooked and sliced from trimmed forerib ex market	43
Topside of beef cooked and sliced from boned and rolled topside ex market	42
Silverside cooked and sliced from salt silverside ex market	60
Saddle of lamb cooked and sliced from trimmed saddle ex market	45
Leg of lamb cooked and sliced from trimmed leg ex market	54
Sirloin cooked and sliced from stripped loin ex market	71
Gammon cooked and sliced from raw gammon ex market	38
Pork loin cooked and sliced from trimmed middle loin ex market	61
Turkey white meat, cooked and sliced from oven-ready whole turkey	35
Turkey dark meat, cooked and sliced from leg of turkey – bone-in	31

Cauliflower cooked from raw cauliflower ex market	41
Beans French sliced from beans French whole ex market	84
Carrots cleaned from carrots ex market	74
Celeriac cleaned from celeriac ex market	61
Lettuce leaves cleaned from lettuce ex market	58
Marrow peeled from marrow ex market	71
Lobster cooked meat from lobster breakers ex market	23

Method of calculation:

Beans French @ £1.40 per lb

$$£1.40 \times 100 = £140.00$$
$$- 85 \text{ (yield)} = £1.65 \text{ per lb}$$

The next step is to cost the recipes fully and to continue to do so at regular intervals to see how costs are changing. Here is an example of costings for a speciality chicken dish over a period of six months.

Sample Recipe Costing

1. MENU   Restaurant
    DISH   Chicken St Katharine
    DATE OF COSTING   January 1993
    DATE INTRODUCED   January 1992

Prep items	Qty	Unit cost	Item cost pence
Chicken breast ex 4½ lb bird	1	sgl	88
Gruyère cheese	1	oz	16
Parma ham (95% yield)	½	oz	12
Egg/breadcrumb mix	1	oz	04
Demi-glace	2	floz	05
Madeira wine	½	floz	10
Trimmed button mushrooms (85% yield)	1	oz	07
Cooking oil	½	floz	02
Artichoke hearts (9 ex 11oz tin)	2	sgl	19
Tomato *concassé* (50% yield)	1	oz	10

PREPARATION COST	173
ADDITIONAL COST @ 5% (see note)	8.65
DISH COST	181.65
PRESENT SELLING PRICE EX VAT	680.85
CASH PROFIT	499.20
% PROFIT	73.3%
COSTED BY (CHEF)	

2.   MENU   Restaurant
        DISH   Chicken St Katharine
        DATE OF COSTING   July 1993
        ALTERATIONS TO
        RECIPE: NIL

Prep items	Qty	Unit cost	Item cost
			pence
Chicken breast ex 4^1/$_2$lb bird	1	sgl	95
Gruyère cheese	1	oz	19
Parma ham (95% yield)	^{1}/$_2$	oz	14
Egg/breadcrumb mix	1	oz	04
Demi-glace	2	floz	05
Madeira wine	^{1}/$_2$	floz	11
Trimmed button Mushrooms			
(85% yield)	1	oz	08
Cooking oil	^{1}/$_2$	floz	02
Artichoke hearts (9 ex 11oz tin)	2	sgl	19
Tomato *concassé* (50% yield)	1	oz	10

PREP COST	187
ADDITIONAL COST @ 5% (see note)	9.35
DISH COST	196.35
PROPOSED SELLING PRICE EX VAT	723.40
CASH PROFIT	527.05
% PROFIT	72.9%

COSTED BY (CHEF)

NB: The prices in this example do not necessarily reflect current market prices.

Once the basic cost of ingredients has been worked out additional allowances must be made for:

- Normal waste in the kitchen
- The provision of rolls and butter and any other 'free items' such as *amuse-gueule*
- The cost of staff meals.

This is usually taken as an extra 5 per cent on the total cost.

Gross operating profit

The next step is to decide on the gross profit margin needed to pay the wages, the variable and fixed costs, plus some profit for the owners and some to plough back into the business. This decision will very much depend on what assumptions have been made in the business plan.

The gross profit can be calculated either by using a cash gross profit uplift or by using a percentage gross profit. With cash gross profit a fixed sum is added to the cost of the dish; with percentage gross profit a fixed percentage of the selling price ex VAT is added. Thus a portion of smoked salmon costing £1.50 may be priced at £5.91 ex VAT with cash gross profit of £4.26 with a 72.1 per cent gross profit.

Some businesses plan their menus on the basis of one; some on the other. Percentage gross profit is particularly popular with accountants but there are some disadvantages in using this method.

- It sometimes restricts the items that can be put on the menu because it can make the high cost items too expensive. Smoked salmon and champagne could be good examples in low to medium spend restaurants (see below).
- It restricts the opportunities for increasing value for money. A number of dishes could be cheaper with a cash profit system.
- It pays no attention to maximising volume by going for cash rather than percentage, ie might even sell it!
- Achievement of a percentage gross profit does not necessarily mean that cash profit target has been reached (see pages 102–107).

The percentage may look good but the overall profit may have been less than you anticipated. An expensive item such as salmon or champagne may look as though it will yield a good return by a percentage mark-up, but if the price is set so high that no one buys it you earn nothing. Far better to set a lower price with a reasonable cash gross profit return and sell the lot. After all, you cannot bank percentages, only cash profit. An example of the contrasting figures is given below.

Examples

If the overall target percentage gross profit on the wine list is 65 per cent, a bottle of moderate champagne costing £12 would have to sell at £34.04 excluding VAT (£40 including VAT). If the champagne did sell the cash profit for each bottle would be £22.04.

If the cash profit on still wine ranged between £8 and £12 giving an average cash profit of £9, a £22.04 profit on champagne might be considered excessive. It might, therefore, be better to decide what is an acceptable cash profit rather than an acceptable percentage profit. A slightly higher cash profit than the highest still wine profit would be sensible and the comparable costings might be as follows.

(a) Looking for 65 per cent gross profit

Cost	Cash profit	Sell ex VAT	Sell inc VAT	% Profit
£12	£22.04	£34.04	£40.00	64.7%

(b) Looking for a reasonable selling price with an acceptable cash profit which will sell

Cost	Cash profit	Sell ex VAT	Sell inc VAT	% Profit
£12	£13.11	£25.11	£29.50	52.2%

So now the selling price is reasonable, the cash profit is acceptable and is better than for the best still wine, but the percentage gross profit has dropped to 52.2 per cent. In this case the cash profit is more important than the percentage gross profit.

It will not be possible to achieve the same cash gross profit on every item for each section of the menu and normally there will be a smaller yield on starters and sweets than main courses. Some dishes are traditionally able to yield a slightly higher cash gross profit than others but at the same time may yield a lower percentage profit. And some dishes give a high percentage profit but a lower cash profit, particularly when there is a limited price ceiling to certain dishes – vegetarian, for example.

(a)   Two dishes with similar cash gross profits but different percentage profits

Cost	Cash gross profit	Sell ex VAT	Sell inc VAT	% Profit
Grilled Dover sole:				
£4.95	£9.51	£14.46	£17.00	65.8%
Blackened red snapper:				
£3.35	£9.42	£12.77	£15.00	74.0%

(b)   High percentage profit dish on same menu with lower cash profit

Vegetarian dish of the day:				
£2.44	£8.62	£11.06	£13.00	78.0%

The aim is to have more dishes on the menu which the customer is prepared to buy and which have above average cash gross profit than those with a lower level of cash profit. Over a period of time, good selling dishes with low cash profits can either be slowly eliminated or the dishes can be altered in such a way as to ensure that the popularity remains but the cash profit increases.

Value for money is important as a selling tool and it is perfectly possible to make more money costing a menu at 68 per cent gross profit overall rather than 70 per cent gross profit overall, simply because more customers might think that the lower gross profit menu is better value and more of them come.

On the other hand, you have to be careful not to sell at 68 per cent gross profit if the same number of customers will come if you sell at 70 per cent gross profit. To begin with, the decision will be based on trial and error and perhaps looking at what other successful restaurants do – later on it will be your own experience that counts.

Planning the menu on the basis of cash gross profit focuses attention on the number of customers or covers and the cash profit per customer. It allows value for money to be increased and ensures that the marketability of the menu is taken into account.

If profit target is achieved the percentage gross profit may still be lower than anticipated. However, it is important not to lose sight of the percentage gross profit because comparing the percentage gross profit achieved against the plan or budget and general industry norms can be helpful in controlling the business.

The combination of cash profit and percentage profit – to control the business – is important. One should not be used to the exclusion of the other; otherwise wrong decisions will be made.

Another important factor in setting the selling price of a dish is the price the customer is prepared to pay. Customers have expectations based on previous experience and what they consider value for money. Sometimes this works in favour of the operation and sometimes against and there will be a mixture of both. The skill is to devise a menu that does not have the most popular dishes with the lowest cash profit, but does have popular dishes with the best cash profit particularly if customers are prepared to pay a premium on items such as smoked salmon, grilled sole or fillet steak. It is important to get the balance right.

Final checks

Before finally deciding that the menu or menus you have created are sound, check that they are interesting, manageable, balanced, saleable and, all things being equal, have a good chance of yielding the required amount of profit to cover all the costs, leaving a profit and reserve to reinvest in the business.

Once the final list of dishes has been agreed, draw up a notional popularity list per 100 customers. The list should include:

- Cost of each item
- Selling price exclusive of VAT
- Cash profit exclusive of VAT
- Percentage profit
- Total number of customers served for each dish
- Total cash sales for each item.

Then calculate:

- The expected number of each starter, main course, sweet, coffee/tea to be sold to 100 customers
- The percentage gross profit for each of the above categories and for the sum total of these categories
- The cash gross profit for each of the above categories and for the sum total of all the categories.

As the expected sales mix will mean a fair amount of guesswork it should be done two or three times taking in different combinations of likely sales mixes. This will not only produce better average figures from which to work but will also give an indication of the effect of movement in sales patterns on the cash and percentage gross profits.

Doing the calculations

Cash gross profit

Cash gross profit is the monetary element which is left after deducting the cost of food *used* from the total sales excluding VAT (revenue) for the period under review.

To calculate the weekly cash gross profit take the opening stock figure, ie the value of the amount of food you started the period with. (The opening stock is always the same figure as the closing stock for the previous week.)

To the opening stock add all the week's food purchases (plus kitchen liquor items). The total purchases figure is obtained from the goods-in control document. (Food purchases do not include non-food items – greaseproof paper, doilies etc.)

Then subtract the closing stock figure – obtained from the stock sheets. What remains is the cost of sales figure, the value of the food actually used.

This cost of sales figure is then subtracted from the sales figure excluding VAT (revenue), obtained from the daily revenue document, to obtain the cash gross profit.

Example

Opening stock	3,075	
Add food purchases	12,201	
	15,276	
Deduct closing stock	3,100	
Cost of sales (food used)	£12,176	
Sales (revenue) ex VAT	39,277	100%
Deduct cost of sales	12,176	31.0%
CASH GROSS PROFIT for week	£27,101	69.0%

NB: The opening stock figure for the next week is £3,100.

Percentage gross profit

Comparison with other weekly results is shown more easily in percentages. Cash gross profit is divided by the sales figure excluding VAT and multiplied by 100.

Example $\dfrac{£27,101 \times 100}{£39,277}$ = food gross profit 69.0%

Percentage cost of sales: To complicate matters, some operations work on percentage cost of sales figures instead of percentage gross profit figures. Whichever is used the two figures should always add up to 100%.

Cost of sales percentage

To be able to compare various weeks' cost of sales figures, they must be converted to a percentage.

Divide the cost of sales figure by the sales figure excluding VAT and multiply by 100.

Example $\dfrac{£12,176 \times 100}{£39,277}$ = cost of sales 31.0%

Cost of sales percentages vary for different types of catering businesses. Here are the trade norms. They are not exact but give an indication of the kind of differences to expect.

50% of sales excluding VAT for pub catering (= 50%% gross profit)
40% to 32% high spend restaurant (= 62–68%% gross profit)
32% to 28% medium–low spend restaurant (= 68–75%% gross profit)
32% to 25% outside catering (= 68–75%% gross profit)

Menu costings I

	COST PER PORTION	SELL PRICE INC VAT	SELL PRICE EX VAT	GP CASH EX VAT	GP% INC VAT	SALES PER 100
STARTERS						
JUMBO PRAWN COCKTAIL	1.40	5.95	5.06	3.58	70.8	20
GAME PÂTÉ EN CROUTE	0.86	4.50	3.83	2.97	77.5	6
SMOKED SALMON	1.81	6.95	5.93	4.10	69.4	15
SEASONAL MELON WITH GINGER SORBET	1.33	4.95	4.21	2.88	68.4	12
SNAILS WITH PUFF PASTRY	1.12	5.95	5.06	3.94	77.9	2
FRESH NORTH SEA SOUP	1.25	4.95	4.21	2.96	70.3	5
AVOCADO WITH CRAB MEAT	1.36	5.25	4.47	3.11	69.6	13
SOUP OF THE DAY	0.53	3.95	3.36	2.83	84.2	18
						91
MAIN COURSE AND GRILLS (INC VEG)						
DUCK WITH ORANGE/COINTREAU SAUCE	4.52	16.25	13.83	9.31	67.3	6
SALMON WITH RHUBARB/GINGER SAUCE	2.54	13.95	11.87	9.33	78.6	10
KING PRAWNS PAN FRIED	4.42	16.50	14.04	9.62	68.5	9
BREAST OF CORN-FED CHICKEN	3.50	14.25	12.13	8.63	71.1	8
LOIN OF LAMB	2.70	14.50	12.34	9.64	78.1	4
VEGETARIAN DISH OF THE DAY	3.45	12.95	11.02	7.57	68.7	2
BEEF WELLINGTON	3.81	17.50	14.89	11.08	74.4	7
FILLET STEAK (8oz)	4.18	16.50	14.04	9.86	70.2	10
SURF AND TURF	4.79	16.50	14.04	9.25	65.9	8
DOVER SOLE (DAILY PRICE)	5.48	16.95	14.43	8.95	62.0	12
SIRLOIN STEAK (8oz)	3.01	14.50	12.35	9.33	75.6	11
LAMB CUTLETS	2.52	13.95	11.87	9.35	78.8	6
MIXED GRILL	3.03	14.75	12.55	9.52	75.9	7
						100

Menu costings I

	COST PER PORTION	SELL PRICE INC VAT	SELL PRICE EX VAT	GP CASH EX VAT	GP% INC VAT	SALES PER 100
SIDE ORDERS						
FRENCH FRIES	0.15	1.25	1.04	0.91	85.8	25
SAUTÉD OR NEW POTATOES	0.19	1.25	1.06	0.87	82.1	20
MIXED SALAD	0.96	3.25	2.77	1.81	65.3	15
GREEN SALAD	0.89	3.25	2.77	1.88	67.9	2
						62
DESSERTS AND CHEESE						
CHOCOLATE/ORANGE MOUSSE	1.37	4.95	4.21	2.84	67.5	9
SWAN MERINGUE	1.40	4.95	4.21	2.81	66.7	1
DEEP FRIED ICE CREAM	0.81	4.25	3.62	2.81	77.6	7
APPLE FLAN WITH ICE CREAM	0.72	4.25	3.62	2.90	80.1	6
SUMMER PUDDING	0.93	4.50	3.83	2.90	75.7	11
TROPICAL FRUIT SALAD	1.11	4.50	3.83	2.72	71.0	6
SELECTION OF CHEESES	0.93	4.95	4.21	3.28	77.9	5
						45
COFFEE AND TEA						
COFFEE AND PETITS FOURS	0.69	2.75	2.34	1.65	70.5	65
TEA AND PETITS FOURS	0.50	2.75	2.34	1.84	78.6	5
						70

Menu costings II

	AV % PROFIT	AV COST OF SALES %	AV CASH PROFIT £	COVERS SERVED	TOTAL
STARTERS AND SALADS	73.3	26.7	3.29	91	299.39
GRILLS AND ENTRÉES	71.5	28.5	9.41	100	941.00
SIDE ORDERS	86.0	14.0	1.25	57	71.25
DESSERTS	74.4	25.6	2.89	45	130.05
COFFEE AND TEA	71.1	28.9	1.66	70	116.20
TOTAL	74.5	25.5	18.5		1,557.89

Example of full menu costing for a medium to high spend restaurant

The costing table shows for each dish the individual cost, the selling price with and without VAT, the cash gross profit, the percentage gross profit and sales mix per 100 diners.

The second chart shows for each section of the menu the average percentage gross profit, the average cost of sales, and the average cash profit, as well as the total sales value per 100 diners.

Observations
1. Game pâté has low sales with a small cash gross profit although a good percentage gross profit, but consideration should be given to finding an alternative dish – maybe a duck pâté with a higher cash profit.
2. Melon with ginger sorbet has a small cash gross profit, a low percentage gross profit with moderate sales; the price should be increased as it obviously has a following.
3. Snails with puff pastry has a high cash profit with low sales, so consideration should be given to finding an alternative dish or lowering the price. If this is decided, the cash profit should not go much below £3.58 which is the cash profit for the most popular starter.
4. There is a good spread of main course sales apart from the vegetarian dish, which should probably remain on the menu even though it will only be taken up by a minority.
5. Dover sole as priced gives a lower than average cash profit and a low percentage profit and is too cheap. The sole is a popular dish and can command a premium price. The cash profit should be a minimum of £9.86 which is the second highest cash profit.
6. Beef Wellington is probably overpriced even though it will also stand a premium price. By reducing it slightly to the same price as the grilled fillet steak it could produce a drift from the fillet steak to beef Wellington. If beef Wellington is priced the same as fillet steak the restaurant will make more money as the cost price of beef Wellington is 37p less.

7. Swan meringue is not selling and consideration should be given to a replacement.

In some ways a properly run outside catering company has a financial advantage over a restaurant operation because cash flow can be assessed well in advance.

You will know the numbers you are catering for before the event and, provided you have a reasonable source of part-time staff, you will be able to provide just the right number of staff to run the functions economically. In a restaurant operation you will often have to guess the volume of customers on any given day, and events beyond your control such as the weather could affect the number.

You should also be able to purchase and prepare the right amount of food to cater for a particular party without any undue waste as the menu will be known in advance. But you need to think ahead as the costings that you are preparing, say, six months in advance may be different from the actual cost of the ingredients at the time of the function.

You will know the cost of overheads and such items as tenting, entertainment and music, and hire of furniture and equipment should have been agreed at the time of the order.

Purchasing

Brian Ridgway

The purchase of materials and equipment is an important element in the day-to-day operation of a catering business and the purchasing policy needs to be clearly defined.

Purchasing policy must answer the question of who will be responsible for purchases. The size of the business is likely to be the deciding factor here. Large companies may well have specific purchasing officers or managers. In smaller companies the general manager or the owner may be the purchaser with the chef in charge of food purchases.

At whichever level responsibility lies, it is essential that all employees know who is in charge. Any limitations on that responsibility also need to be defined. For example, day-to-day food purchases may be left to the chef, while one-off purchases of expensive equipment may be the responsibility of the general manager.

The purchasing policy should also set out the type, quantity, standard and amounts of materials and equipment to be purchased in the form of purchasing specifications. It will also look at the type of suppliers to be used and include setting up and controlling ordering, receiving and payments systems.

Food purchases

Quite detailed decisions will need to be made, particularly in the purchase of food. For example:

- Where is the quality level to be set?
- Are frozen foods permissible or is everything to be bought fresh?
- Will every dish be made from scratch or is there to be a degree of ready prepared ingredients?
- Are baked goods to be bought in or made on the premises?
- Is the meat to be bought by the portion, joint or side?

- Is fish to be bought whole or filleted?
- Are vegetables to be rough or prepared?

In answering these and many more detailed questions reference must be made to the menu and style of food. The following factors must also be taken into account.

- The price to be paid per item with any possible discounts
- The labour involved in producing from scratch with an analysis of wages
- The availability of skills among the chefs
- The convenience of ready-to-use ingredients and products
- Simplification of portion control with the use of prepacks
- The quality of the prepared product with reference to menu policy
- Customer expectation and acceptance
- The variety available and the need for changing menus
- The available storage space.

Once the basic decisions have been made and a list of required goods has been drawn up, the next stage is to make out detailed purchase specifications.

Purchasing specifications

In a small restaurant or catering company the purchasing specification may simply cover the quantity and quality of the required product, such as 5kg unblemished Bramley cooking apples or four large legs of English lamb with the skin in place. But as the business grows in complexity and the number of covers or customers to be supplied increases, more detail will be required.

A good product purchasing specification needs to cover quality level and country of origin; quantity, size and weight; thickness, cut and ratios (meat to bone); colour, style and shape; maximum/minimum tolerances; packaging and delivery factors.

The value of such a detailed specification is that it plays a vital part in providing a standard product with a minimum of waste at the correct and expected cost. It eliminates communication problems. Everything is set down on paper and the specification acts as an *aide-mémoire* to all concerned of what was agreed.

The catering establishment has a record of what was ordered and the suppliers know what is required and cannot get away with supplying sub-standard goods on the basis that they were not quite sure what was ordered. All goods can be checked easily on delivery.

The specification can be sent to a number of different suppliers for quotations and the results can be directly compared. Even the smallest of businesses can benefit from some formalisation of their purchasing.

The example from a large hotel group given below may be too detailed for smaller operations but it serves to highlight the points which should be considered by all businesses.

Sample meat specifications with general conditions
Meat specifications
General conditions

1. *Source of supply*
All meat purchased for supply to . . . must be obtained from EEC approved abattoirs, or companies with a minimum grade B under the MLC hygiene inspection scheme.

2. *Transport*
All vehicles used for the delivery of meat must be refrigerated. They must be clean, free from any infestation and residue from the previous day's deliveries and shall comply with all food hygiene regulations currently in force in this country.

Meat must not at any time during preparation or delivery be allowed to come into direct contact with the floor. Fresh meat, cooked meat and poultry should always be kept in separate containers from each other.

The driver must take all necessary precautions to ensure that the highest standards of hygiene are applied to the meat, the vehicle and him/herself. Clean overalls and suitable head covering must be worn at all times by drivers when delivering or handling foodstuffs.

3. *Temperature*
At no time either during preparation or delivery should the temperature of fresh meat rise above 5°C, or below −2°C. Frozen meat must be delivered at a temperature of −18°C, unless requested otherwise.

4. *Frozen meat*
Any meat which has previously been frozen and thawed for any purpose must be clearly identified by an attached label stating 'DO NOT REFREEZE'.

5. *Boneless meat*
Boneless meat must be weighed and priced *after the bones have been removed*. The bones must not be included in the weight invoiced or accompany the meat when delivered to the hotel.

6. *Butchery*
All meat must be butchered strictly in accordance with the following cutting specifications or where specified the Meat Buyer's Guide for caterers' specifications. Any muscle containing unnecessary incisions, causing undue wastage, will be rejected. (See item 14.)

7. *Additives*
We do not accept meat from any animal treated with hormones or chemical tenderisers.

8. *Packaging*
All identified cuts of meat should be vacuum packed with the seals intact. The vacuum should be tight on the meat to minimise blood loss. Packs supplied with excessive blood loss will not be accepted. Each pack must be clearly labelled with all the following information:

(a)   Date when packed

(b)   Use by date. A minimum of 7 days' shelf life is required on receipt at delivery point

(c)   Quantity/numbers (eg 5 × 8oz; 2 × 16oz)

(d)   Name of cut

(e)   Country of origin

(f)   Net weight of contents. (Packaging must not be included in the weight supplied.) Any cuts not requested vacuum packed must be wrapped in 'peach paper' or another suitable covering.

All packs to be transported and delivered in plastic trays or new cardboard boxes.

9.   *Times of delivery*

To be during the opening hours of the kitchen and by arrangement with the chef, normally between the hours of 8 am and 2 pm. Any deviations from these times to be notified before delivery.

10.   *Invoices/Delivery notes*

Goods delivered to establishments must be accompanied by a delivery note/invoice which gives a full and proper description of the cut and type of meat delivered, the weight, country of origin, price per pound and total price. The weight delivered must be reasonably accurate to that ordered. The company will not accept responsibility for goods left on its premises unless the signed (legible) receipt is obtained from a person who is authorised to accept deliveries.

Statements must be submitted to . . . at the end of every month. The current terms of trading are payment 60 days from statement.

11.   *Alternatives*

No alternatives will be accepted without the prior agreement of . . . In the event of supplies not being available at the time of delivery, the supplier shall immediately inform the hotel, in order that alternative arrangements may be made.

12.   *Prices*

All nominated butchers will quote prices on a weekly basis.

13.   *Other conditions*

Free access to the suppliers and their supplies premises shall be granted to any accredited representative of . . . at any reasonable time.

All suppliers to the company are required to be either members of the National Association of Catering Butchers, or submit to a full inspection by a nominated agent of . . . .

14.   *Rejected goods*

A senior member of the . . . staff may reject goods at the time of delivery if in their opinion the goods are not to the company's specification. Immediately the supplier receives notification, he shall, at his own expense, remove the rejected goods, and shall not redeliver these to . . . The supplier will immediately replace all rejected items with acceptable goods, if required.

15.   *Expenditure*

Suppliers will, if requested, supply . . . with details of the value of purchases made by the hotels during a given period.

16. *Improper inducement or reward*

Employees of . . . are not allowed to accept money or goods from any supplier. Any company found offering such incentives, whether accepted or not, will immediately have their nomination withdrawn.

17. *Legislation*

All deliveries made under this agreement shall conform to the relevant legal requirements currently in force in this country.

Beef Specification
Fore-rib (Oven Prepared)

Carcase type   Fresh
United Kingdom/Eire

Cut removal To be removed from the brisket by a cut not more than two inches (50mm) from the ventral tip of the eye muscle. To be removed from the middle rib between the fifth and sixth rib. To consist of five ribs, both face cuts to be parallel.

Trim level Chine and remove dorsal vertebrae. Cut down feather bones to expose the ligamentum nuchae (paddy wax). Remove same together with scapula gristle and associated muscles. Peel back fat cover (brisket end) to expose first muscle attached to underside and remove. Flatten out fat cover to an even thickness. Trim away all exposed blood vessels and discoloured tissue.

Fat level External fat thickness not to exceed half an inch (12mm). Any internal fat deposits not to exceed half an inch (12mm) in diameter.

Preparation Tie securely between ribs, replace feather bones and tie with two strings.

Packaging To be individually vac-packed with bone guards on rib ends.

Weight range Small 11–13lbs; Large 14–16lbs.

Chicken Supreme Specification

Carcase type British

Cut removal To be boned from the breast leaving wing intact.

Trim level Remove the first two outer joints of the wing leaving one wing joint containing humerous bone.

· ALL SKIN AND FAT TO BE REMOVED

Packaging To be vacuum packed in 5s.

Weight range 6, 7 or 8oz +/− ¹/₂oz.

NB: Specify weight when ordering.

Fish Specifications

Fresh salmon whole (Scotch)

Weight to be 8–10lb excluding head and after cleaning. Cleaned fish to have roe cavity and offal chambers completely excised and head to be removed parallel with gill fins. No spent or gaffed fish will be accepted.

Salmon Darnes

Weight 5oz and 7oz. Bilateral tolerance ½oz. Ex 8–12lb cleaned weight fish. No tailend portions accepted.

Dover sole whole

Cleaned weight 14oz. Bilateral tolerance ½oz. Black skin to be removed, gill cavities and roe chamber to be thoroughly cleaned. Tailfin and fringes to be removed.

Dover sole fillets

Ex 14oz cleaned weight fish. No spent fish to be used. Both for whole fish and fillets, Dutch or English preferred.

Suppliers

Goods can be purchased from retail or wholesale outlets or from cash and carry stores. Small businesses will probably use a mixture of local retailers and cash and carry. Orders are not usually large enough to interest wholesalers but they may be large enough to negotiate a discount from a good retailer.

Purchases from cash and carry stores have increased over the last 15 years and much of this increase has come from small businesses. Prices are favourable. Cash is paid on the spot and the transaction is completed then and there.

However, there are advantages and disadvantages to this method of purchasing.

Advantages

- A whole range of products can be bought at the same time and under one roof.
- There is no problem with minimum order levels although most items will be in catering packs rather than packed individually.
- Stock levels, and therefore capital outlay, can be kept to a minimum.
- Prices will be less than most retail prices.

Disadvantages

- Prices will not be as keen as those from a specialised wholesaler.
- Volume purchases are not normally taken into account.
- There is generally no delivery service.
- Cash has to be paid then and there, so no credit is available.
- Although there is a range of different types of goods, it is unlikely that the cash and carry will stock a wide range of fresh fish, meat, fruit or vegetables. Such items are more likely to be frozen.

Large operations may well decide to make their own arrangements with specialist wholesalers and small businesses may prefer to shop around giving orders for items such as fresh fruit, vegetables, meat and fish to a variety of suppliers. Another relatively new option is to join a buying consortium (see page 116). This can make large savings on dry goods.

Whatever the mix of suppliers decided upon it makes sense to investigate produce and service claims thoroughly. Are they consistent? Even if an investigation gives a satisfactory result it is a mistake to get locked into one particular supplier. If you do prices can rise alarmingly.

If possible choose local suppliers and get to know them. Start by visiting their premises to check them out, not least from the hygiene point of view, and then start to build up a relationship by asking for opinions, recommendations and tips. Invite them to eat in the restaurant – they may even become regulars and spread the word!

The better the relationship with suppliers, the more smoothly the operation will run. Here are some ways of making the purchaser/supplier relationship work more smoothly. They apply as much to liquor and general purchasing as to food purchasing.

- Forecast ahead to give the supplier an idea of likely demand over six months. This also allows more accurate ordering over the short two- to four-week period. The benefit is that the kitchen avoids running out of items which might cause disappointment to a customer without too much capital being tied up in large stocks in the store-room. This is particularly important if the item is not available from the supplier on a day-to-day basis but has to be specially ordered.
- Ensure that the supplier can meet the optimum product specification.
- Make sure suppliers realise that goods delivered must be exactly to specification and that any changes in quality or price must be disclosed prior to delivery.
- Ensure that the supplier knows at what time and which date goods are required.
- Consider after-sales service and follow-up as part of the overall decision not just price alone.

Liquor purchases

Large catering concerns and companies at the top end of the market will employ their own specialists or hire consultants to plan the wine list and purchase wines and spirits. This will be out of the question for the smaller restaurant and caterer. Nevertheless, these businesses must still offer their clients a comprehensive choice of drinks.

Suppliers range from small local shops to the big national brewers. Wine can also be bought direct from the vineyard. The choice will depend upon the quantities required, the available storage space and the amount of capital which can safely be tied up in this part of the business.

It is worth remembering that operating on a fairly low stock level has the advantage of minimising cash flow problems and of keeping expensive mistakes to a minimum.

Retail outlets and cash and carry. Small catering companies with a low turnover in drink will probably find that they cannot afford to buy in bulk from wholesalers. Supermarkets and off-licence chains now offer an excellent range of reasonably priced wines which will be suitable for most occasions. Off-licences such as Oddbins and Threshers probably have the edge as they will offer discounts on wine by the case. They will also deliver within their own catchment area.

Cash and carry outlets can supply bottled and canned beers and a wide range of spirits at good prices. An account can be opened for regular purchases. Cash and carry stores also stock wine but the quality is not usually very good.

Wholesale wine merchants. Wholesale wine merchants vary in size considerably. Large companies can offer continuity, competitive prices and regular deliveries. Some of them will help with the planning of the wine list and keep managers up to date on trends and fashions in the wine world. In some cases the merchant will supply a complete cellar stock, invoicing the business for replacement stock as it is ordered. The cellar stock remains the property of the supplier.

The disadvantage of this kind of arrangement is that the restaurant or catering company is tied to the supplier until such time as it is prepared to pay for the stock holding. Buying solely from the big companies can also be rather restricting. The wine is usually reasonably good but not distinctive.

Smaller suppliers often specialise in particular regions and this can be useful for restaurants specialising in a national cuisine or with a regional theme of some kind. It is also easier to build up a closer relationship with a smaller supplier who might well take a more personal interest.

The location of the supplier is less important than size and speciality but proximity may be useful for faster deliveries or emergency replacements. A balanced and interesting wine list may need to have its wine sourced from more than one supplier and a mix of well-priced basic wines from one of the larger wholesalers, together with some more interesting and unusual wines from a couple of smaller merchants, could work well.

Breweries. Breweries will normally be the best supplier of draught beer and they may also be able to supply a range of bottled beers, spirits and wines through their associated wine merchants. Some of the considerations on size outlined above will also apply here.

Auctions. Auctions are useful for buying large quantities or conversely for buying extremely small parcels of fine wines or spirits. They are therefore suitable both for large catering companies and for restaurants which want to include a small number of fine wines on their lists.

One of the advantages of buying at auction is that wines and spirits can be bought at competitive prices. The disadvantage is that there is no guarantee of being successful. The auction itself can be daunting. This is a specialist area which should be approached with caution.

Buying direct. This can be done by visiting the wine-growing regions and tasting the wines at the vineyards. However, this is time consuming and it is possible to buy direct without leaving the country. The various wine growers' consortia and the shippers hold annual or bi-annual tastings in London where owners and managers can taste the wine and make arrangements to buy at ex-cellar prices. Shipping costs, VAT and excise duty are paid separately to the shipper.

Buying wine in this way may mean that there is a delay between tasting and ordering and the final delivery of the wine. However, it does also mean that the wine can be stored in bond until such time as it is required to replace existing stock. This can help the cash flow of the business as taxes and duties are not payable until the wine leaves the bonded warehouse.

More importantly, direct buying offers the opportunity to buy the very best wine in each price range from a region rather than pay a merchant a premium for possibly inferior wines. If you get it right you can keep the same margins and offer very good wine.

Non-food purchases

All catering establishments will need to purchase non-food and beverage items such as kitchen equipment, pots, pans and utensils; cleaning materials; printing and stationery; and laundry. Restaurants, pubs and hotels will need to add restaurant and bar equipment; china, glass and cutlery; and silverware.

Many of these items can be bought individually by going to the cash and carry for the smaller day-to-day items and direct to suppliers for larger orders or large one-off purchases. However, it is unlikely that you will be able to negotiate anything much better than the normal trade price. Larger purchases are just not possible for small businesses with erratic cash flow and limited storage space.

However, hotels, restaurants and outside catering companies which do not belong to a group or chain can join a buying consortium, such as Prestige Purchasing administered by LMS (Consultants) Ltd. These groups are able to use the combined buying power of all their members to negotiate much larger discounts than those members could achieve on their own.

Membership is by a fixed fee but this should be recovered quite quickly. The greatest savings are usually to be made on high volume goods used regularly such as cleaning materials but dry goods and drinks can also do well. Membership of a consortium can also be useful to obtain keener prices on wallpaper, soft furnishings, carpets and furniture when refurbishing and consortia can also advise on, and purchase, insurance.

There are currently at least four main purchasing consortia in the market but there is a tendency for them to change. All should be thoroughly investigated before any decision is made to join. It is vital to have a fairly accurate idea of the items you will wish to purchase and the quantity; also what they would cost elsewhere. The consortium will charge a membership fee so it is vitally important that the savings made are more than the fee.

Cost control

Effective cost control takes in a good information system, knowledgeable bulk buying, careful negotiation and a good monitoring system. It also means being thoroughly *au fait* with current prices. Most suppliers issue regular price lists, particularly for perishable goods or for products whose price can fluctuate considerably.

Use up-to-date price lists as a basis for both comparison and evaluation. Compare the list prices of at least three suppliers (see the sample Supplier Quotation Comparison on page 119) and if possible play one supplier off against another, but check that all suppliers are quoting on the same product specification. (See pages 109–113.) It is useful to keep all price lists up to date but even more useful to build up your own records.

Arrange a weekly call-over of the prices of all perishable goods and log them. In this way a history can be built up of the comparative performance of individual suppliers: who is the cheapest, who is the most consistent and so on. This information may help in future negotiations, and it will also help the manager to monitor the decisions of those responsible for purchasing if this has been delegated.

Regular monitoring is an important part of effective cost control. Compare the purchase prices of all goods with price indices, price lists in trade papers and magazines, and keep up the check against other suppliers' lists.

All these records enable a picture to be built up of the availability and supply lead time for critical ingredients. Lists of goods with advantageous prices at particular times of the year can be drawn up and used as an aid to keeping costs down when choosing menus ahead of time. Trade journals (see page 237) can be useful in this area and should be monitored regularly.

In addition to their regular prices most suppliers offer special prices, deals and apparent bargains. Some of these, such as seasonal prices, are quite genuine; others may seem good value but may only be made possible by substandard quality.

Occasionally there are naturally occurring gluts; some national, some local. These can create real bargains but a sample should be obtained before buying in quantity. Never be tempted into a quick decision. Buying at the cheapest price is not necessarily the best policy – quality may be below standard or wastage high.

General discounts for bulk buying can look attractive but the advantage may be lost if it results in orders in excess of requirements. This risks deterioration and wastage; less space for other goods, especially if kept under refrigeration, and increased work in record-keeping. It is also short sighted if security is weak or the business does not have the facility to store the product in good condition. There may also be a minimum delivery drop which would make bulk buying impossible for the smaller company.

When all facts have been monitored it is time to start negotiating. Don't just accept prices the way they are; haggle and shop around for bargains. Remember, suppliers love 'soft' customers – they can walk all over them. Try to drive as hard a bargain as you can.

SUPPLIER QUOTATION COMPARISON

SUPPLIER

A = MEAT FOR YOUR PLC
B = BUTCHERS CONSORTIUM
C = FRESH MEAT CO
D = BULLY BEEF CO

ITEM	UNIT	WEEK 1 / / PRICE PER LB				WEEK 2 / / PRICE PER LB				WEEK 3 / / PRICE PER LB			
		A	B	C	D	A	B	C	D	A	B	C	D
Forerib	10–14lb	246	220	242	235	240	225	244	236	248	230	245	238
Rump steak S	6oz	388	390	395	380	398	395	380	390	409	395	380	390
Fillet steak S	6oz	717	720	722	715	864	830	850	835	864	830	840	850
Lean Mince S	2lb	110	108	98	112	156	128	130	140	156	128	130	140
Leg of lamb NZ	5–7lb	202	190	207	196	130	135	146	141	138	140	150	145
Pork chops HK	6oz	148	145	129	137	148	150	149	145	148	160	155	152

Simply placing the order and monitoring cost levels is not enough to ensure an efficient purchasing system. Controls must cover ordering systems, receiving systems and payment systems (see pages 43–56).

Ordering procedures

Controlled ordering is essential to ensure that the correct goods are delivered on time and according to specification. The overall responsibility must rest with the owner/manager, food and beverage manager or chef. Day-to-day ordering may be carried out by other employees but it should always be based upon agreed policies and procedures.

The level of authority will, of course, vary according to the size of the business and suppliers should be informed of who is authorised to place orders and what to do if this is ignored.

- Always use agreed suppliers unless specific permission has been given and agreed, and maximum stock levels adhered to.
- Avoid standing orders for daily or weekly deliveries, particularly for perishable food. Both requirements and prices may change. Standing orders are hard to cancel at short notice and can easily lead to excessive stock holding and wastage. Shortages, too, can occur when relying on regular deliveries causing emergency and possibly more expensive purchases to be made.
- Check all holding areas for stock of all products before reordering. This should include refrigerators as well as freezers and store rooms.

Maximum stock levels are usually equivalent to about five to seven days' consumption for food and 30 days for liquor. The least stock held the better – provided that service to the customer is not adversely affected.

Experience will dictate the general levels of stock required for most foods but reference to anticipated increases or decreases in demand, local or national events, foreseeable problems and even the weather forecast can be useful.

Where possible suppliers should be given written orders on pre-printed and numbered order forms signed by the person responsible. Confirm all telephone orders and on-spec van sales in writing and hold copies of all orders until after delivery and payment.

The order should include clear and precise details of the items required together with their product specification, agreed price, delivery date and time, and any special points that might need to be noted. The written record of orders provides for an accurate record of all these points and should ensure a low level of deviation from the order requested.

One method of avoiding over-ordering on non-perishable items is to order a par-stock level. Thus if a product ordered by the dozen reduces to six then six more are ordered or if reduced to four, eight more are ordered. The level is kept at 12. The parstock level can be changed from time to time according to the level of business.

Over-ordering does not help the business as it will mean that cash is tied up in unwanted stock for which there is a risk of deterioration and wastage. There will

OFFICIAL ORDER	D417952

(COMPANY NAME, ADDRESS AND TELEPHONE NUMBER)

TO: (SUPPLIER)

DATE:_____

Please supply and invoice to the following:

If in doubt contact: Tel:

Please quote the number of this order on Advice/Delivery note and invoice

QUANTITY	DESCRIPTION	COST
	INVOICE TOTAL LESS DISCOUNT PLUS VAT AT CURRENT RATE	

COMPANY NAME, ADDRESS (OF REGISTERED OFFICE) AND REGISTRATION NUMBER

Authorising signature: ....

DAILY/WEEKLY ORDER SHEET

Week commencing   /   /

ITEM	Unit	MONDAY				TUESDAY				WEDNESDAY			
		Supplier	Price £	Qty ord.	Qty del.	Supplier	Price £	Qty ord.	Qty del.	Supplier	Price £	Qty ord.	Qty del.
Rump steak	lb	FF	3.40	10lb	10lb								
Calf liver	lb	FF	4.80	7lb	8lb								
Dover sole, 14oz	lb	Y	4.80	8.75lb	9lb								
Lump fish roe	jar	Y	1.50	24	24								
Celery	head	SPC	0.55	6	6								
Lettuce, cos	ea	SPC	0.43	15	15								
Mint sauce	jar	BF	2.22	6	6								
Raisins, 3kg	bag	BF	3.33	1	1								

be less space remaining for other goods, particularly if it has to be refrigerated and there will be increased work in record-keeping.

Delivery and receiving procedures

The delivery and receipt of goods is one of the areas in food and liquor control which is particularly vulnerable. There can be both accidental and deliberate malpractice leading to serious stock losses with adverse gross profit results. Aspects of food hygiene must also be considered carefully.

After accepting goods as being 'as ordered' it is not possible to go back to the supplier later to complain without a great deal of difficulty (and sometimes ill feeling). For this reason it is important to establish a strict routine for the receipt of goods and for that procedure to be adhered to at all times. Any deviation could be construed as a breach of discipline.

First of all, specific employees should be made responsible for the safe receipt of all goods. If goods are going straight into a production or service area it will probably be the chef or head of department who carries out the checking process.

If they are dry goods or liquor the storeman or cellarman will do the checking. In smaller companies one person may be in charge of checking all deliveries. The control systems in a large organisation should ensure that those who have placed the order regularly inform those who are to receive the goods.

DAILY/WEEKLY ORDER SHEET

THURSDAY				FRIDAY				SATURDAY				SUNDAY				TOTAL
Supplier	Price £	Qty ord.	Qty del.	Supplier	Price £	Qty ord.	Qty del.	Supplier	Price £	Qty ord.	Qty del.	Supplier	Price £	Qty ord.	Qty del.	

No goods should be accepted or signed for without checking against a copy of the order for all aspects of the specification. It is useful to have copy orders visually displayed awaiting the arrival of an order.

A double check on the price and quality specification can be useful. On occasions when such a check is not possible the delivery slip should be signed with the words 'contents not examined' or 'contents unexamined'.

Others points to cover include:

- Always weigh or count bulk products precisely; never estimate or guess. If goods are short delivered the delivery note should be marked with full details of what has been received and a credit note requested. Both the person who gave the order and the supplier should be contacted and informed of the shortfall.
- All goods should be examined by a competent member of staff who is able to verify acceptable quality. Items which do not come up to specification must be refused. It is particularly important to check the 'use by' details as the Food Labelling Regulations 1989 prohibit items being on the premises after the 'use by' date.
- Malpractice is a problem with certain delivery men so every carton or container must be checked to see that it has not been tampered with. Odd items can easily be removed without this looking obvious.

- Never leave goods unattended and if night or weekend deliveries are necessary extra attention may need to be given to ensuring that the goods are secure after delivery.
- Only sign delivery notes for goods which have been delivered. This sounds obvious but some delivery men are skilled at getting signatures for goods which are *expected* to be delivered later in the day. Another sharp practice is for delivery men to return goods to the van while the delivery notes are being signed.

Certain aspects of the Food Hygiene Regulations and the Food Safety Act 1990 also apply when accepting foodstuffs. In this connection the following points should be checked.

- Goods in damaged packaging or containers should themselves be checked for damage.
- Badly dented or rusting cans should be rejected as should punctured vacuum packs.
- The interior of food delivery vehicles should be inspected for cleanliness and any dubious circumstances reported.
- All uncovered or open perishable food except fruit and vegetables should be rejected.
- Open food which comes into contact with the floor or ground while being delivered should be rejected.
- Food delivered in refrigerated lorries should be sampled and checked for the correct temperature. Use a probe thermometer to check the temperature at the centre of the sample item and record it in a book kept at the entrance to the goods receiving area. If the temperature for frozen goods has risen above $-16°C$ or $5°C$ for chilled goods, report it to the suppliers. If nothing is done to improve the situation, consider changing supplier. If no action is taken and there is a food poisoning problem, the company could be deemed not to have acted with due deligence. (See page 71.)

Storage and Stock Control

Brian Ridgway

This is an integral part of the line manager's job. Bad storage conditions and procedures have an adverse effect on the standard of food and drink sold. This in turn results in the operation failing to achieve the required cost and profit targets.

Storage conditions

Different types of commodities will require separate storage conditions in order to maintain, and in some cases improve, their condition and quality before being served to the customer. These commodities are split into the following general categories. Check the Food Hygiene Regulations for the correct temperatures at which to store certain foods.

Meat

Meat yet to be matured and butchered must be hung in a cold room at a temperature of 0–1°C with space between to allow free circulation of air and with drip trays below to catch any blood. According to the type of meat it should be hung for a period of 3–14 days to allow for the chemical changes to take place which produce tender meat. Hung and butchered meat can be purchased ready to cook and this should also be stored at 0–1°C.

Poultry and game, if undrawn, should be stored at 0–1°C with the exception of venison, hares and rabbits which should be hung at 3–4°C. Drawn or eviscerated poultry should be stored on slatted shelves at 0–1°C, and game placed on metal trays at the same temperature.

Fish

Fish must be stored in a separate special type of fridge with perforated non-rust trays, allowing fish to drain and permitting easy cleaning. Place the fish on crushed ice on a wet cloth covered with another cloth and crushed ice and store at 1°C. Place shellfish in boxes covered with wet sacks and crushed ice and store at a temperature of 3°C (not lower). Wet fish and shellfish should be stored for the minimum period of time and there must be a careful system of rotation.

Fresh fruit and vegetables

All types of fruit and vegetables should be stored in a cold room with no direct sunlight into or on to the outside of the room. The room must be dry and well ventilated with bins for root vegetables and racking for other types. Because fruit and vegetables deteriorate quickly, there must be space to rotate the stock properly. Bananas and pineapples should be hung. Soft fruits and melons should be refrigerated at 1–2°C.

Dairy produce

Dairy produce with the exception of cheese should be stored in a refrigerator or cold room at a temperature of 3°C. Milk must be kept covered as it will absorb strong smells such as fish, onions and cheese. Butter and eggs too will absorb smells if not well protected.

Most whole cheeses should be stored in a cool, well-ventilated area, but soft cheese (whether whole or cut) which has been ripened by the action of moulds or other micro-organisms must be stored at a temperature not exceeding 5°C, together with all other cheeses that have been cut or otherwise separated from the whole cheese.

Frozen foods

Frozen foods keep in a freezer with a minimum temperature of −18°C. Stack on plastic coated trays or baskets. Most foods should be properly defrosted before use. Ice-cream can be stored at −12°C for immediate use but at −18°C for long-term storage.

Tinned food and dry goods

Store in a dry, well-ventilated place. Inspect regularly for rusting, bulges (ie blown tins) caused by gases from either bacteria or the tin plating being attacked by the food. If this happens the tins *must* be thrown away. Use dented tins first before they rust and puncture.

Keep all loose commodities in bins with lids. Some products such as tea, coffee and rice should be stored in containers with tight lids. Other items like bread, flour and sugar should be kept in tins with loose fitting lids. Goods with strong aromas should be stored away from those items that are likely to absorb flavours.

Liquor store, wine and beer cellar

All alcoholic drinks should be stored in a room with a constant temperature which should be automatically controlled. Wines must be racked horizontally to preserve quality. Spirits and liquors can stand upright on shelves. Bottled beer and minerals can be stored in their crates in a stacking area of the room or sometimes in a separate room.

Draught and keg beers should be kept in a separate air conditioned store with easy access from the dispense area, so that barrels can easily be changed when required. This separation also helps to maintain the security of the wines and spirits as barmen are often allowed, indeed, expected to change barrels.

Empty bottles and crates are worth money too and a secure space should also be provided for storage until collected. Managers often make the mistake of forgetting about the security of empties, resulting in a monthly deficit.

Cleaning materials
A separate store is required because of the strong smells and the dangerous substances used. The store should be dry and well ventilated with slatted racking. The Fire Precautions Act should be consulted when dealing with inflammable materials. (Incidentally this also includes spirits.)

Storage operation
Here is a checklist for the efficient and hygienic operation of the stores areas:

- Choose an area which has an easy flow in and out and which is adjacent to both goods entrance and kitchen.
- Ensure that the correct lighting and temperature control is installed and that the area is dry and well ventilated.
- Avoid foods becoming contaminated by incorrect storage or by loose waterproof coverings dripping on to the food below.
- Ensure that the areas are well organised with space for the rotation of stores and with items easily visible for stock taking.
- Ensure that all areas and fridges and freezers are cleaned regularly and that walls, floors and shelving are constructed of easy-clean materials.
- Set up a pest-reporting system so that all sightings are dealt with immediately. Rats, mice, cockroaches and birds should all be eliminated as quickly as possible and steps taken to avoid a recurrence.
- Establish good security, possibly with security cameras and an issue counter.

Stores procedures and records
The condition of the stores is important but store records are just as important.

- Record details of all goods into store.
- Record details of all goods out of store.
- Keep records on bin cards or store ledger cards for each item in the store.
- Carry out regular stock taking and spot checks, particularly of high value items. The bin or book stock must equal the actual stocks.
- If there is a store or cellarman, keep him informed with forecasts of the stock levels he should work to.
- Keep inventories of small equipment and fittings in each area of the operation and check the lists every quarter.

- Record all old equipment out and new equipment in and keep a record of the serial numbers of high value items.

Caterers who have built up a stock of in-house equipment for use at outside events should institute the same kind of check-out, check-in procedures for this equipment.

Stock taking and stock valuation procedures

Careful stock taking and equally careful valuation of stock from the stock sheets are essential in calculating the cost value of the food used and the food percentage gross and cash profit for any period. Any errors will result in inaccuracies in the food gross profit results.

Stock taking is also useful in providing checks on:

- Stock that needs to be used up quickly
- Unmarked or unlabelled stock which should be thrown away
- Food hygiene standards within the stores
- Prices and the amending of costing cards
- Total stock carried and the amount of capital tied up in the business.

The most usual interval for stock taking is one month. Ideally, it should be carried out after business on Sunday evening. The larger the operation, the more frequent the need for a stock take and this may mean weekly checks.

Accurate stock taking is one of the most labour intensive tasks in the food control cycle. For consistent results the job should be done by the same person each time. In some operations it is the job of the food and beverage controller, in others the chef.

The person who undertakes the stock taking task must be totally familiar with the layout of the dry stores, the location of all fridges and freezers, and be aware of other stock holding areas such as shelves and cupboards. A consistent route cuts down on the chance of missing stock put in unusual places.

Reduce mistakes by careful attention to the following points:

- Use standard dated and numbered stock sheets which include every food item in the stores and kitchen or in the cellar if it is to be a liquor stock take. Some stock sheets have additional columns for seasonal or one-off items.
- Check the top 25 cost items first. They are the most important, they are the most attractive to steal and they will lose the operation the most amount of money.
- Look out for items which are split between two or more locations and make sure that all areas are covered.
- Never guess the weight, volume or number of any item. Guesswork on high priced items can easily create inflated or undervalued stock.
- Arrange for all deliveries to be made after stock taking.
- Record the correct size and price based on the last delivery of the item. Some prices vary daily so make adjustments for any price increases.
- Carry out the valuation as speedily as possible so that if an investigation is required it is done as soon after the stock period as possible.

Double check the stock sheets for errors if the valuation of the stock shows an unusual result or if the food gross profit result or the food gross profit percentage is in variance.

As a final check compare the stock summary sheet with the previous period and develop a gut feel for silly errors.

STOCK CONSUMPTION

WEEK COMMENCING: /   /

ITEM	Unit	Price £	Open stock	Receipt	Close stock	Consumption	Value £
Rump steak	lb	3.40	2lb	60lb	3lb	59lb	200.60
Calf liver	lb	4.80	1lb	45lb	2lb	44lb	211.20
Dover sole, 14oz	lb	4.80	2.6lb	60lb	3.50	59.1	283.68
Lump fish roe	jar	1.50	5	24	18	11	16.50
Celery	head	0.55	2	35	4	33	18.15
Lettuce, cos	ea	0.43	4	90	6	88	37.84
Mint sauce	jar	2.22	2	6	6	2	4.44
Raisins, 3kg	bag	3.33	.5	1	.75	.75	2.50

Management Operating Manuals

Brian Ridgway

Operating manuals are an essential management tool. They ensure that everyone knows what to do, how to do it, when to do it and to what standard. They also ensure that employees work consistently in the same agreed manner. Company policies, styles of operation and standards are set down for all to see. In addition, operating manuals can be used as the basis for selection when recruiting, for training schemes and for reviewing performance.

To be effective manuals must cover *all* procedures and standards in detail from the time employees commence their shifts until the time they go home. They must also cover all employees including management. This kind of detail is bound to result in a great deal of paperwork even for a modest operation and the manual will be quite thick and forbidding. To get over the problem of distributing such a large document most operations split it into a number of small manuals dealing with different areas of the business such as:

(a) Kitchen preparation and still room staff covering daily duties and responsibilities, recipes and cooking methods, standards of presentation, dress code, health, safety and hygiene practices, fire prevention and fire drill in the event of a fire, house rules and use of equipment. (See pages 133–134.)

(b) Restaurant and outside servicing staff covering the daily duties and responsibilities, methods of service of each item on the menu and wine list presentation, customer contact, bill checking and cash procedures, dress code, health, safety and hygiene, fire prevention and fire drill in the event of a fire, use of equipment and relevant licensing laws. (See pages 136–144.)

(c) Administrative staff covering purchasing, ordering, goods receiving, systems, food and beverage control, accounting, relevant legal requirements and codes of practice, personnel and training, and use of equipment such as boilers, air conditioning and electrical equipment.

As the operation grows and responsibilities are delegated, it will probably be necessary to write separate manuals for the main administrative disciplines.

Some entrepreneurs argue that compiling a manual for a small business is a waste of time. Once written and the initial euphoria over, it will end its days at the bottom of a pile of papers in a desk drawer. There is, of course, a danger of this but the discipline required to write such a manual certainly concentrates the mind on many details which are likely to be forgotten without it. Once written the manual will at least serve as an *aide-mémoire* and at best can become a vital tool in achieving consistency and maintaining standards.

Catering companies employing freelance chefs and service staff may not need to use quite such comprehensive manuals but it is still important to be able to quickly outline the duties required of each batch of staff as they are hired. Simple written sheets outlining duties may be all that is needed.

Running the Kitchen and Food Preparation Areas

Brian Ridgway

There are a number of different ways in which the kitchen may be organised and these will depend upon:

- The complexity and size of the menus
- The number of times a menu is changed and the number of daily or weekly supplementary items
- The volume of customers
- The days and hours of opening
- The method of service.

The staff may consist of the head chef with one or more of the following additional posts: sous chef, chef de partie, commis chef, kitchen porter.

The head chef is the kitchen manager and his responsibilities include:

- The total management of the kitchen, still room and wash-up area
- The compilation of menus
- The standards of cuisine
- The ordering of foodstuffs
- The training of staff
- Recommendations for capital equipment and day-to-day kitchen equipment
- The profitability of the kitchen operations.

The duties of the second chef or first sous chef include:

- Deputising for the head chef when he is not on the premises
- Supervising detailed administrative work such as work rotas, training records, health and safety records

- Possible responsibility for outdoor catering if relevant or banqueting or the smaller of two restaurants if there is more than one.

The duties of the chef de partie include:

- The charge of a section of the kitchen depending on the size of the operation but he could be in charge of the sauce, fish, larder, vegetable, soup or sweet sections of the kitchen. A chef de partie should be capable of taking over any section of the kitchen in the absence of any of the other chefs de partie.

The commis chefs are assistants to the chefs de partie. In a large restaurant there may be first and second commis chefs in each section.

In addition, there may be a kitchen clerk, a small number of kitchen porters and still room attendants according to the size of the operation.

The kitchen clerk, apart from helping with all the clerical duties, will often be required to stand at the hotplate and call out the orders as they are received in the kitchen. Alternatively, the head chef or the first sous chef will carry out this task. It is, in fact, an important job as the person doing this is, in effect, controlling the production line and is also the quality controller. He checks every single item before it is handed to a waiter.

The Food Hygiene Regulations affect all kitchen areas and it is of paramount importance that the provisions of the regulations should be adhered to at all times. Here is a checklist of some of the points to watch:

- All foods should be kept covered to prevent contamination and dehydration.
- All foods for hot service must be kept above 63°C. However, if this temperature is exceeded by too great a margin the food will dehydrate and become unusable.
- All foods for refrigeration or freezing must be properly and quickly cooled and held at the correct temperature. Blast chillers are recommended for joints of meat or cooked food in bulk.
- Foods frozen on the premises should be clearly labelled as such with product name and production/freezing date.
- Leftovers should be used with care. If in doubt discard at once.
- Only reheat food once. Any such reheating should be done thoroughly and quickly. The reheating temperature should reach 82°C.

A complete list of the appropriate legislation is given in Section 3.2 on pages 71–73.

Washing up

The dish-washing process is extremely important and adequate training must be given to staff working in this area to ensure a hygienic and efficient operation. China items, serving dishes and cutlery should be dealt with separately from glass and from pots, pans and utensils.

Glass washing is also important and can be done totally manually, partly manually by placing glasses on rotating brushes or in a machine similar to the normal dishwasher, but especially designed for glassware.

Try to avoid total handwashing of china, cutlery and glass as it can be unhygienic. The wash water becomes progressively dirtier, the rinse water also, and the drying cloth becomes wetter and wetter. It is also more difficult to finish an article to the required presentational standard manually. To do so is a slow process and operators become bored and lose concentration.

Spending some time training a new recruit properly for washing-up duties of all descriptions is well worth doing and will reap benefits. It is a crucial task and untold problems will be caused if it is not done properly.

4.8

Transporting Food

Brian Ridgway

The vehicles used for transporting food must conform to the Food Hygiene Regulations (Dock Carriers) 1960 Amended, and the 1966 Food Hygiene (Market Stalls) and Delivery Vehicles 1966 (Amended) and the Food Hygiene (General) Regulations 1970.

The vehicles should be viewed as an extension of your kitchen and preparation area, particularly for the transportation of 'open' food that is not sealed in packaging material.

Internally the vehicles should:

- Be constructed of non-porous easily cleanable surfaces and have no uncleanable crevices
- Be kept spotlessly clean at all times
- Be refrigerated for the transportation of foods that are required to be kept refrigerated to prevent them from spoiling or because the foods are relevant foods in the new Regulation 12 of the 1966 Regulations and must be transported at a temperature below 5°C

- Be insulated to reduce the possibility of contamination from outside sources such as exhaust fumes, smoke, extreme heat or cold, birds, insects and vermin.

At the very least the back of the vehicle must be separated from the driver's cab to minimise contamination from that area by cigarette smoke, dust and dirt, open windows and heat from the heater.

4.9

Running the Food Service

Brian Ridgway

Whatever the decisions on the style and standard of service they must be efficiently communicated to the management and staff working in food service. In a restaurant these decisions, once taken, remain permanently in place but with an outside catering operation they are more likely to be made by the client. It is essential to be sure that everything is agreed in advance.

In some ways running an outside catering company is like opening a restaurant every day or, in the case of event catering, every three to seven days. Each event needs to be treated as a military operation. Good administration and detailed planning are essential. There are no second chances or opportunities to make a second choice as there are in a restaurant. Everything has to be provided on the right day at the right time and in the right numbers.

If the customer has ordered a particular dish for 200 people six months ago, he or she expects 200 portions of that dish on the day and not 175 with alternatives for the other 25. Every eventuality has to be thought about and decisions taken on how to overcome any problems which might occur without the backing of an ongoing restaurant operation. Experience counts for a lot.

Often outside catering companies are asked to organise much more than just the food and drink. Here is a checklist for an elaborate function such as a wedding or an important product launch.

Sample checklist

- *The budget*. Decisions on everything else depend on the prospective spend.
- *The location*. Does the client have a prospective location or does he or she want help with this? The chosen location must be checked out, particularly if a marquee is to be erected or if the cooking is to be done on site. Check the access, availability of power points, cooking appliances, space for preparation and space for the event itself, availability of fridge and freezers, washing-up arrangements and distance of the preparation area from the service area. Are there parking facilities?
- *Equipment required*. This may include any of the following: tables and chairs; public address system for speeches; cooking and chilling equipment hire; crockery, cutlery, glasses and serving platters, linen, barbecue equipment.
- *The staff*. Bookings must be made well in advance for butler, bar and waiting staff, chefs, kitchen staff and washer-uppers. Is a master of ceremonies, doorman or security staff required? Will a photographer be required? Is transport required to get staff to inaccessible locations?
- *The food and drink*. Full details of the style of meal must be agreed in advance and the menu chosen. Is there a need for any special diet food? Accompanying drinks, special drinks for toasts, water, tea, coffee, soft drinks and bar details must also be agreed. Do you need to order a special cake?
- *The layout of the service area*. How is the food and drink to be served? Consider access points to a buffet table and the provision of tables and chairs. Is a top table or dais required for speakers? Are flowers required and do the tables or the room need to be decorated? Is there to be a seating plan and will printed menus be required?
- *Timing of the event*. An outline timetable of the event including set-up times, guests' arrivals, food and drinks service, speeches or presentations, duration of the event and the estimated conclusion will be extremely useful.

Once the service decisions have been agreed for an event or in a restaurant, the following areas must be considered and covered in procedure manuals, instructions to staff and training sessions.

Duties of staff prior to service

In the one- to two- hour period before service commences serving staff usually lay up the sideboards and tables and fill cruets, peppermills, sauce bottles and sugar bowls.

In small restaurants they may also be responsible for cleaning the dining room and for simple food preparation. The latter may include preparing plated side salads, making dressings or melba toast, butters, preparing coffee and tea, setting up cold buffets, sweet trolleys and cheese boards.

PRIVATE PARTY CATERING ORDER FORM

Company name:		Date:				No. of pax		
Address:		Times from:	To:					
		Location:		Signature of approval:				
		Type of event:		Date accepted:				
Organiser:		Guaranteed minimum nos		By:				
		Room hire	Rate	Tel.		Corres.	Pers.	
Telephone: Agent: Account to:		Marquee hire						
Credit: Yes No Type of settlement:		Coffee/Tea breaks am				Price		
		Coffee/Tea breaks pm				Price		

TIME	ACTIVITY	NOS	PLACE	Meals	Nos	Times	Location	Price PP
				Lunch				
				Dinner				
				Menu/Buffet				

Items	Cost	Items	Cost	Drinks
Flowers		Dance floor		At conference:
Candles		Raffle drum		
Menu cards		Balloons		At reception:
Place cards		Music		
Table plan		Photographs		At dinner/lunch:
Conference plan		Entertainment		
Toastmaster		Security		After dinner/lunch:
Staging				
Licence Extension From: To:		Audio/ Visual		Cigars and cigarettes

I have read and agree with the terms and conditions overleaf.

We would remind you that final numbers are required at least 24 hours in advance. Please sign the form, keep the top copy and return the bottom copy to us at the above address.

Signature: Date:

No.

A useful checklist for room preparation by an outside catering company includes:

- Set up buffet table and arrange tables and chairs as required
- Arrange table cloths and lay tables
- Arrange the buffet table or bar and check for easy access of stock and of guests
- Fill all condiment sets, sugar bowls and check the menu for other accompaniments which need to be put into place.

Method of service of all dishes

Staff must know exactly what kind of service is expected. The choice includes:

- Silver service where the food is served by the service staff from serving dishes
- Plate service where all the food is plated in the kitchen
- Combinations of silver and plate where the main dish is plated and vegetables and accompaniments are served by the staff (or left on the tables)
- Family service where the staff present the serving dishes to the customers who help themselves.

Staff also need to know:

- Which size of plates should be used for each dish at each course
- The cutlery to be used for each dish
- The composition of each dish, and the price
- The correct accompaniments to each dish.

Method of drinks service

This is often the responsibility of a specific wine waiter but in small establishments or at a catered event drinks may be served by the general service staff who will need to know which glasses to use and how to serve the aperitifs, wine and liqueurs.

Order of service

Here is a checklist for the efficient reception and service of customers in a restaurant:

- Meet and greet customers as they come in. In larger restaurants this will usually be done by the head waiter but if he or she is not by the entrance this duty should automatically be taken over by whoever happens to be in the restaurant and is nearest to the customer
- Offer drink, water, rolls and butter
- Take the order
- Serve all items of food to the left of the customer and clear from the right
- Serve beverage to the right of the customer and clear from the right
- Serve ladies first
- Never clear until every member of the party has finished eating that course
- Pay regular attention to rolls and butter and refilling glasses
- Offer coffee or tea
- Be on hand to produce the bill.

Duties at end of service

- Ensure that all dirty plates, cutlery, glass are cleared to the wash-up
- Put dirty table cloths and napkins in the laundry basket
- Count the number of table cloths and napkins for the laundry list
- Clear away all condiment sets ready for filling the following day. Empty and soak English mustard pots
- Empty sauces back into main containers so that small containers can be washed
- Hand in bill books and check pads with bill control slip
- Clear away buffet to kitchen where appropriate
- Ensure that sideboards are all clear of rubbish or dirty items
- Switch off lights
- Where 'still room' duties are carried out by the waiting staff, empty and clean coffee-making machinery and serving jugs. Return milk and cream to the refrigerator
- Return biscuits and melba toast to tins
- Return cheeseboards to refrigerator storage
- Generally ensure that the whole area is clean and tidy and ready for the preparation team to start work the following day.

General service

There are a number of other points which should be communicated to staff and which make for more efficient and effective service. They include:

- A cleanliness check on aprons, uniforms, shoes, hands and nails
- Prompt service and good communication with the kitchen
- Never leave the room – or the kitchen – empty-handed. There is always something to clear and always sideboards to refill
- Never leave the room (or the customer's sight) for longer than necessary.

These are the bare bones of the job. Staff will also need to be trained in billing and checking systems (see pages 59–62), cash handling and security (see pages 219–223), communication and sales skills (see pages 184–185), dealing with complaints (see pages 185–186) and handling emergencies (see pages 224–226).

4.10

Bar Operation

Brian Ridgway

The bar should be an important profit centre for any catering operation but it must be carefully planned and honestly run. If not, it will simply be a lucrative base for dishonest bar staff.

Siting the bar

In a restaurant the bar is in a fixed position, usually near the entrance, but at a catered event the bar can be set up in the most convenient place for that function. If it is to be a pay bar, the entrance or an equally prominent site makes commercial sense. At a private function it may be better to site the bar away from the door so that guests are drawn into the room, leaving the entrance clear.

Staff

The choice of bar staff is crucial. They must:

- be *sober*
- be honest and hardworking
- know the licensing laws and stick to them
- know about drinks and mixed drinks
- have a pleasant personality and sell well without being pushy
- be quick and efficient
- have a good telephone manner
- be a good talker with a fund of stories.

Equipment

Apart from the obvious items such as corkscrew, crown cork opener and sharp knife, the most important items on the bar are the measures. These must conform to legal standards. Spirits such as gin, whisky, vodka, brandy and liqueurs must be sold in measures of 1/3/1/4/1/5/1/6th of a gill or 25cl or multiples thereof, using either a standard thimble pouring measure or an optic measure. Metric measures will be compulsory from 31 December 1999.

Draught beer or cider may be sold in multiples of half a pint in a government stamped glass or through a metered pump directly into the container from which it will be drunk. The meter must be visible to the purchaser. Beer quantities will not go metric in the foreseeable future so the good old British pint is probably here to stay.

At present wine can be served in any size of glass but it is expected that legislation to bring in a standard measure will be introduced in the future.

Stocking up

The range of drinks depends on a number of factors:

- Storage space in the bar
- Storage space in the cellar
- Availability of money – capital outlay can be high
- Restaurant feature or theme.

The basic selection list for a mixed bar includes: gin, whisky, rum, brandy and vodka; port, sherry and vermouths; mixers; red and white wine, beer and cider. The basic bar can be augmented by the addition of a range of gins, whiskies, vodkas and the addition of malt whiskies, bourbon whisky, VSOP and XO brandy, champagne, vintage port, liqueurs and ingredients for a range of cocktails.

Once the bar is fully stocked and running the bar staff will need to stock up before each meal session. The whole bar should be checked during this process to make sure that everything is clean and tidy and that everything works properly. New stock should be placed behind old stock to ensure that old stock is used first.

It is important to have a proper system for moving stock from cellar to bar or for moving drinks in and out of a movable bar at a catered event. A checklist for such systems should include the following:

- Record all movements in and out of the cellar
- Use bin cards in the cellar. Give each bin card three columns:
  - (a) stock in
  - (b) stock out
  - (c) signature of the person moving stock
- Do regular spot checks to see that the number of bottles in the bin is equal to the result of the calculation: stock in less stock out.

A similar system should be used to check stock in and out of transit vans and in and out of a temporary bar. Remember to check the empties as well as the full bottles; the latter can be passed off as empties if they are packed into the case upside down. Alcohol is almost as attractive as cash and so signatures on recognised movement documents must be the order of the day.

Service

The decision must be made about whether service is to be to the customer direct or via waiters. Either way, the duties of the bar staff should be laid down in the management manuals.

The staff must know exactly which measures and glasses are to be used for which drinks. They must also know the correct temperatures at which to serve the various drinks, the agreed garnishes and presentation, and, of course, the prices.

The more sophisticated the establishment or the catered event, the more important it will be for bar staff to know the recipes for mixed drinks and cocktails. Even the most unsophisticated bar should have the recipes for the most popular cocktails on hand. These might include Bloody Mary, Dry Martini Cocktail, Champagne Cocktail, Whisky Sour, Pina Colada, Margarita, Sidecar, Manhattan, Planters Punch and non-alcoholic cocktails.

Anyone serving wine must know something about the wines on offer. This becomes progressively more important the larger the wine list and the more sophisticated the restaurant. The wine waiter's job is easier if full details of the wine (including producer or *negociant* and the vintage) are given on the wine list. He should be able to discuss with the customer the relative merits of a traditional claret and a Chilean Cabernet Sauvignon. Ideally, he should also be able to suggest which wines will go well with which dishes on the menu.

Duties prior to service will include stocking and laying up the bar with lemon slices and other garnishes, putting out nibbles such as crisps, nuts and olives or more elaborate canapés. Duties at the end of service usually include washing glasses and cashing and locking up. They may also include cleaning and re-stocking for the next meal.

If the bar is designed to act as a control point for the restaurant the following duties will be added:

- Taking bookings and general enquiries by phone
- Dealing with enquiries at the door
- Meeting and greeting arrivals and looking after those waiting to order in the bar
- Helping with coats
- Setting and monitoring heating and lighting in the bar
- Setting the levels of background music
- Dealing with cash taken at the bar and in the restaurant
- Watching for trouble and trouble-makers.

Good communication skills and selling skills (see pages 184–185) are as important to bar staff as they are to service staff in the restaurant.

Control systems

It is essential to set up systems to cover the following areas and to ensure that all bar staff understand them.

- Billing and checking systems (see pages 59–62)
- Cash handling and control (see pages 219–223)
- Cellar work (see below).
- Handling complaints (see pages 185–186)
- Handling emergencies (see pages 224–226)
- Licensing laws (see page 141 and below).

Cellar work

Looking after a cellar is largely a question of organisation with the possible exception of a real ale cellar which can be more difficult and problematic.

The main points to consider are:

- Sensible layout so that all stock is easily moved to and from its storage area.
- Temperature maintained at no more than 60°C and no less than 15°C. If it is possible, store red wine and spirits at room temperature and white wines and beers at 15°C. This is especially helpful if the dispense bar area is cramped and short of space. It ensures that replenishments from the cellar arrive in the bar at the correct temperature for serving.
- An orderly racking system so that anyone can see at a glance where each item is and can take stock accordingly when deciding what to reorder or for valuation when stock taking. It is embarrassing and inefficient to run out of stock at the wrong time, it is also inefficient and can be costly too to end up with too much stock, both of which can easily happen if it is difficult to locate the contents of the cellar.
- An efficient control system which at the same time ensures that there is just about the right level of stock to match the business and deters theft and pinpoints quickly that stock has disappeared when it should not have done. Control systems need not be over-sophisticated, in fact the simpler the better (see above).
- Draught beer cellars, particularly real ale cellars, are generally separate areas from the dry cellars and require skill to look after the ale. Generally, the brewery firm from whom the ale is purchased will train those responsible as it is quite an art to produce a pint of bitter in first-class condition through a handpump at the bar. The same expertise is not required for keg beers and bottled beers.

Licensing laws

It is obviously essential that the management know the licensing laws in detail. However, it is also important that members of staff who dispense and serve alcoholic drinks also know the relevant section of the laws that immediately affect their work. Any infringement of the laws by the staff can lead to the prosecution of the company, the licensee and the member of staff who caused the infringement.

It is prudent to set down in writing the relevant sections of the law and train the staff to keep within the law. At the same time, they should be informed of both the legal and company penalties that may be involved if they transgress. They should also be compelled to sign a document agreeing that they:

- Have been given a copy of the relevant laws
- Have been given appropriate training
- Know the penalties for transgression.

Detailed instructions should cover the following areas:

- Permitted hours for the service of alcoholic drinks
- The difference between residents and non-residents in a hotel
- Measures to be used – both statutory and non-statutory
- What short measures are
- Dilution and passing off
- Under-age drinking and the purchase of cigarettes
- Drinking-up time
- Betting, gaming and lotteries
- Prostitution.

You may wish to add other important instructions such as:

- Price indication regulations
- Drinking and smoking on duty
- How to deal with gratuities
- Over-ringing/under-ringing cash registers.

4.11

Control of Gross Profit

Brian Ridgway

Having spent a great deal of time and effort on planning and costing the menu and wine list, setting up purchase agreements, designing 'goods-in' and storage systems, agreeing cooking and service methods, and installing accounting systems, it would be foolish to start trading without knowing how you are going to control the food and liquor operation from the time the goods are specified and purchased until the time the resulting turnover goes into the bank account.

So many things can, and indeed will, go wrong if a continuous check is not made on each aspect of the cycle. Although the following diagnostic chart should be used immediately if there is evidence of poor gross profits, it should also be used on an ongoing basis for prevention rather than cure.

Factors affecting   *Causes*
kitchen % GP

Purchasing

1. Suppliers and   (a) Poor specifications
    specifications
                           (b) Supplier unable to cope with volume or
                                standard

                           (c) Accepting minimum deliveries which are too
                                much

                           (d) Not keeping close to the price of goods or
                                shopping around

                           (e) Being taken for a ride or conned

                           (f) Poor response following complaints

                           (g) Poor yields

                           (h) Poor menu planning

2. Ordering   ✓(a) Incorrect specification, quantity, price

                           ✓(b) Over-ordering: resulting in too much stock
                                 using up too much space

                           ✓(c) Disputes about what was ordered

                           ✓(d) Verbal orders without written follow-up can
                                 result in:

Methods of detection

Purchasing

1. Suppliers and
   specifications

   (a) Not fit for the job in hand with regard to
       size, weight, standard, quality so dumped
       or more used than necessary

   (b) As above or let down thus having to
       purchase at short notice from another
       supplier at a higher price

   (c) Food wasted (look in bins)

   (d) Check price lists with competitors and trade
       magazines

   (e) Being over-friendly or simply lax

   (f) Items not changed immediately. Credit
       notes slow in materialising or not at all

   (g) Observation and physically checking

   (h) Poor profitability. Using high priced items
       at wrong time of year

2. Ordering

   (a) Invoice. Visual check

   (b) Stock deteriorating. Stock values too high.
       Recent shortage of storage space

   (c) Incorrect deliveries, prices

Remedies

Purchasing

1. Suppliers and specifications

(a) Re-check all specifications against requirements

(b) Change to more suitable supplier

(c) Agree smaller drops or change supplier

(d) Continually monitor prices from all sources

(e) Don't be over-friendly with suppliers and be able to say no. A good rapport yes

(f) Change supplier

(g) Regularly carrying out yield tests to check they are still valid

(h) Plan menus to take advantage of seasonal items that are cheap. Have a mixture of low cost and high cost basic items

2. Ordering

(a) Tighten up control. Ensure that orders are placed by authorised staff who know what they are doing

(b) Closely monitor levels of business and establish trends. Establish par stocks for non-perishable goods. Eliminate fixed standing orders. Order as frequently as supplier will allow to ensure low stocks and fresh goods

(c) Try to follow up with written order or at least ensure all orders are recorded at the time of the verbal order. Ask the supplier's clerk to read back the order and take the name as a reference

Factors affecting	*Causes*
kitchen % GP	

I (ii) *Materials* lost through delivery

1. Receipts short on delivery

    A) *Quantity not checked* owing to:

        (a) Staff being too busy and not checking

        (b) Staff being indifferent, misunderstood and not motivated

        (c) Staff being unsuitable because of poor selection and wages

        (d) Staff being new, untrained and inexperienced

        (e) Insufficient time

        (f) Staff not following laid down procedures

        (g) Carelessness, accidents

        (h) Dishonesty leading to pilferage and stealing

        (i) Deliveries at the wrong time

    B) *Poor transportation*, bad storage on van owing to:
Points *(a) to (g) above* and:
Incorrect temperatures

    C) *Loading and unloading*, owing to:
Points *(a) to (h) above*

    D) *Credit notes not received*

2. Change in source of supply and quality

    A) *Poor material specification* in the first place

    B) *Changes* in standard not being communicated or checked

Methods of detection

I (ii) *Materials* lost through
delivery

1. Receipts short on
    delivery

A) (a–i) Inspection and observation at delivery
    points. Spot checks at time of delivery
        Unsigned delivery notes or orders
        Security checks
        Comparing weekly issue sheets with
            order quantities received
        Staff turnover
        Questioning staff concerned on their
            knowledge of any laid down
            procedures and knowledge of goods
            ordered

B) Goods arriving when goods entrance not
    manned or very busy
        Visual checks of delivery van
        Log temperatures of delivery vehicle

C) Visual check of loading efficiency.
        Ensure all items are unloaded and
            received

D) Keep a record of shortages or alterations
        Change in source of supply and quality

2. Change in source of
    supply and quality

A) Checking material specifications
        Comparing weekly issue sheets

B) Checking over changes and liaising with
    buyers

Remedies

I (ii) *Materials* lost through
delivery

1. Receipts short on
    delivery

    A) (a–i) Establishing procedures and adhering
        to them for checking order quantities on
        receipt.
        > Constant spot checks
        > Careful selection, training and treatment
        > of staff, ie good management

    B) Agree delivery times with supplier and
        make supplier keep to them.

    D) Follow up records all the time
        > Change in source of supply and quality

2. Change in source of
    supply and quality

    A) Knowing items ordered, material
        specification and quality

    B) Establishing communication procedures
        and adhering to them

Causes

I (iii) *Materials* lost
through storage

1. Incorrect stock levels
    and stock

    A) Over or under-ordering owing to:
    Points (a) to (g) inclusive (page 149)

    B) Incorrectly assessing business expected:
    Points (a) and (h) (page 149)

    C) Poor labelling and use of storage facilities

2. Incorrect place of
    storage and
    temperature

    A) Poor labelling and use of storage facilites
    owing to:
    Points (a) to (h) inclusive (page 149)

    B) Staff rushing to get away at close of
    business

    C) Fridges not inspected or defrosted
    regularly, or temperatures checked
    regularly, poor maintenance

    D) Poor layout and storage facilities

    E) Lack of knowledge regarding storage
    methods

    F) Leaving stores unlocked

Methods of detection

I (iii) *Materials* lost through storage

1.	Incorrect stock levels and stock	1. (A–C) Inspection and observation of storage areas and facilities, at close of business

1.   Incorrect stock levels and stock   1.   (A–C) Inspection and observation of storage areas and facilities, at close of business
Spot checks on storage areas
Comparing weekly stock sheets
Questioning staff concerned on their knowledge of any laid down procedures and knowledge of stocks and storage areas

2.   Incorrect place of storage and temperature   2.   (A–F) Inspection and observation of storage areas and facilities
Spot checks at close of business or before start of next day's business
Staff turnover and wages sheets
Questioning staff concerned on their knowledge of any laid down procedures and knowledge of storage areas
Hygiene observed
Stores unlocked

Factors affecting   *Remedies*
kitchen % GP

I (iii) *Materials* lost through
storage

1.	Incorrect stock levels and stock	1. (A–C) Establishing procedures and adhering to them for stock taking and stock levels Providing labels for marking stock properly Constant spot checks Careful selection, training and treatment of staff, ie good management
2.	Incorrect place of storage and temperature	2. (A–F) As above. Ensure all goods are properly stored at the close of business Take regular temperatures of all fridges and log. Ensure regular fridge maintenance Review storage facilities Ensure tight security of stores areas

Factors affecting kitchen % GP	*Causes*

I (iii) *Materials* lost through storage

3. Poor stock rotation ✓   A) Failure by staff:
                                                   Points (a) to (g) inclusive (page 149)

                                                 B) Poor layout and storage facilities. Lack of space. Poor lighting

4. Breakdown of plant ✓   A) Failure by staff (either own maintenance staff or maintenance contractors):
      Points (a) to (g) inclusive (page 149)

     B) Not logging fridge temperatures daily

     C) Repairs not carried out quickly enough

5. Fridges left unlocked ✓   A) Failure by staff:
      Points (a) to (h) inclusive (page 149)

     B) Responsibility not assigned for keys

     C) Poor locks on fridges etc

     D) Repairs not carried out quickly enough

6. Hygiene ✓   A) Failure by staff:
      Points (a) to (g) inclusive (page 149)

Factors affecting kitchen % GP	*Methods of detection*

I (ii) *Materials* lost through storage

3. Poor stock rotation

3. (A–B) Inspection and observation of storage areas and date stamp items. Spot checks on storage areas. Questioning staff concerned on their knowledge of any laid down procedures and knowledge of stocks and storage area

4. Breakdown of plant

4. (A–C) Inspection and observation of storage area equipment, in particular fridges. Spot checks on storage areas. Questioning staff concerned on their knowledge of any laid down procedures and knowledge of equipment storage area

5. Fridges left unlocked

5. (A–D) Inspection and observation and of storage areas. Spot checks, particularly overnight
    Questioning staff

6. Hygiene

6. Regular inspections.
    Questioning staff on their knowledge

| *Factors affecting kitchen % GP* | *Remedies* |

I (iii) *Materials* lost through ~~delivery~~ Storage.

3. Poor stock rotation	3. (A–B) Establishing procedures and adhering to them, ie regular inspection Careful selection, training and treatment of staff, ie good management Review layout
4. Breakdown of plant	4. Establish procedures Regular maintenance of fridges Staff to report and record all wastage Set up fridge temperature checks on a daily basis and log
5. Fridges left unlocked	5. (A–D) Establish procedures, checking at end of service Maintain tight security
6. Hygiene	6. Establish procedures Ensure all know hygiene regulations

Factors affecting *kitchen % GP*	*Causes*

I (iv) *Materials* lost through usage

1. Wastage in kitchen

A) Over- or under-ordering
Points (a) to (h) inclusive (page 149)

B) Over- or under-preparation
Points (a) to (h) inclusive (page 149)

C) Over- or under-portioning
Points (a) to (g) inclusive (page 149)

D) Poor or bad cooking
Points a) to (g) inclusive, including cooking and hot storage at incorrect temperatures causing shrinkage

E) Incorrect recipe
Points (a) to (h) inclusive (page 149)

F) Incorrect use of leftovers

G) Accidents
Points (a) to (h) inclusive (page 149)

H) Altering standards used, ie quality

I) Change in raw material leading to reduction of standard yield from item concerned

Factors affecting kitchen % GP	*Causes* Methods of Detection

I (iv) *Materials* lost through usage

1. Wastage in kitchen

A) Spot checks, inspections, observation of service areas, either random or routine
Particularly at end of business
Questioning staff concerned on their knowledge of any laid down procedures
General atmosphere and commitment

B) As above

C) As above as well as taking samples and weighing them

D) As above as well as tasting food and eating in restaurant

E) As above as well as routine checks on standard yields and recipes

F) As above

G) Accident statistics

H) Checking issue sheets, recipes and observation

I) Refer back to purchasing specifications and check yields

Factors affecting kitchen % GP	*Remedies*

I (iv) *Materials* lost through usage

1. Wastage in kitchen

A) Establishing routine procedures and control systems and adhering to them, eg on order levels and quantities
    Constant spot checks
    Forecast business
    Careful selection, training and treatment of staff, ie good management

B) As above, plus preparation on demand or small quantities and replenish
    Ensure banqueting and private catering numbers are confirmed

C) As above as well as providing correct ladles, sample portion sizes, visual aids and portion scales

D) As above and follow up training

E) As above, on site check by management

F) As above

G) As above
    Staff to record all wastage

H) Training

I) Constantly check adherence to specifications

Factors affecting kitchen % GP	*Causes*

I (iv) *Materials* lost through
usage

2. Misappropriation of   A) Unauthorised consumption by staff
   materials

   B) Removing materials from premises
      Stolen when not under supervision either
      during hours of trading or at night when
      materials are not locked up. See storage

Factors affecting   *Causes*
kitchen % GP

I (iv) *Materials* lost through
usage

2. Misappropriation of   A) Observation. Spot checks
    materials

                                 B) Observation
                                     Using security staff to bag search
                                     Checking stock between meals or
                                     overnight

Factors affecting kitchen % GP	*Remedies*

I (iv) *Materials* lost through usage

2. Misappropriation of materials

A) Giving staff opportunities to eat wholesome staff food

Commitment of supervision to policy and not turning a blind eye to illicit consumption

B) Security checks. Staff bag searches. Check stock at close of business and first thing next morning to see if stock has disappeared overnight. Check consumption against waiting staff order checks and customers' bills

Factors affecting kitchen % GP	*Causes*
II *Cash* lost as a result of	
1. Mistakes	A) Failure to include items on bills *Points (a) to (g) inclusive*
	B) Failure to extend items on bills *Points (a) to (g) inclusive*
	C) Mistakes in addition of bills
	D) Changes in selling prices not communicated or forgotten
2. Fraud and mistakes	A) Presenting a bill more than once
	B) Not recording the cash on the accounting machine
	C) Not presenting the correct bill, or any bill, or just presenting a receipt
	D) Recording sweet items in the bar part of a bill to obtain extra drinks for own consumption
	E) Adding to the bill in pencil and then rubbing out or adding to the receipt. Pocketing cash
	F) Altering bills – should only occur through participation of management
	G) Customer walking out without paying
	H) Issuing bills to friends who come in and not collecting cash – or not issuing a bill at all

Factors affecting kitchen % GP	*Causes*

II *Cash* lost as a result of

1. Mistakes

1) (A–D) Reduction in average spend per person
     Observation by management
     Spot checking of bills during and after meals
     Random checking and comparison of average bill and cash from each waitress/waiter
     Special attention to bills of new waitresses/waiters
     Questioning of staff concerned on their knowledge of any laid down procedures
     Routine or random checks of key items by relating consumption to sales (involving analysis of bills)
     Shortage of cash against till totals

2. Fraud and mistakes

A) As above

F) Use special pens for alterations

G) Missing bill or till with cash missing

H) Observations. Not issuing food unless an order check is made out or authorised by management

Factors affecting kitchen % GP	*Remedies*

II *Cash* lost as a result of

1. Mistakes

1) (A–D) Establishing and adhering to routine procedures and methods of detection
    Constant spot checks
    Careful selection, training and treatment of staff, ie good management
    Use of security agents to test purchase

2. Fraud and mistakes

A–E As for mistakes
    Avoiding using a pencil
    General vigilance
    Bill control using sequential numbering
    Observation
    Discipline
    Dismissals

F) All alterations to be in special pen with manager's signature

G) Bill control. Waiting staff and cashier to be vigilant

H) Checking procedures

Factors affecting kitchen % GP	*Causes*

III *Clerical* errors in results

1. Poor communication leading to misunderstanding	A) Foods not cross-charged to other departments if more than one
	B) Misunderstanding of facts
	C) Wrong prices used
	D) Poor writing, ie illegibility
	E) Incorrect recipe or costing
	F) Failure to carry out procedures in respect of goods
2. Arithmetical errors	A) Misreading of figures, ie reversing
	B) Multiplication errors
	C) Addition errors
	D) Wrong column
	E) Incorrect units for prices
	F) Wrong turnover figures used

Factors affecting kitchen % GP	*Methods of detection*
III *Clerical* errors in results	
1. Poor communication leading to misunderstanding	1) A–F Systematic checking going on in office, investigating weekly results Getting original sheets Aware of cost prices, look at recipe and compare with issue sheets Improve communications Watch for careless employees
2. Arithmetical errors	2) A–F As above

Factors affecting kitchen % GP	*Remedies*

III *Clerical* errors in results

1. Poor communication leading to misunderstanding	1) A–F Familiarising oneself with the way one's results are calculated Checking major areas of cost using one's restaurant experience to identify mistakes not immediately apparent Ensure clear communication Training to correct carelessness
2. Arithmetical errors	2) A–F As above

Factors affecting kitchen % GP	*Causes*

IV *Other factors*

1. Poor stocktaking

        A) Missing stock

        B) Incorrect count

        C) Incorrect calculations

2. Function business not credited to stock period — Late making up of function bill

3. Follow up credit notes — Lack of system

4. Change in sales mix

        A) Change in season

        B) Change in customer type

        C) Change in menu and prices

        D) Change in selling effort

Factors affecting kitchen % GP	*Methods of detection*

IV *Other factors*

1. Poor stocktaking	1) A–C Review by chef Check obvious mistakes Spot check
2. Function business not credited to stock period	2) Proper numerical bill control and return to accounts clerk for inclusion in accounts
3. Follow up credit notes	3) Record all credit notes owing at time of agreement with supplier that credit is due ie on the day and at the end of the accounting period
4. Change in sales mix	4) A–D Expect changes in the sales mix from time to time so monitor continually

Factors affecting *kitchen % GP*	*Remedies*
IV *Other factors*	
1. Poor stocktaking	1) A–C Same stock takers each time as far as possible Spot checks on major items Instigate and monitor system Review disciplines, authorities and responsibilities Regular training and follow up React quickly when problems have been identified; delay means loss of profit
2. Function business not credited to stock period	2) As above
3. Follow up credit notes	3) Instigate log book and follow up system
4. Change in sales mix	4) A–D Record monthly sales mixes

Although some of the checks and remedies outlined above are applicable to liquor control as well as food control, there is also a simple control check which can be used to see that you are getting the right return from the bar and wine operations.

Take opening stock value; add the deliveries; take away closing stock and you are left with the consumption. Value the consumption at selling price excluding VAT. Compare this figure with the cash take excluding VAT. The two figures should be the same. If they are not, something is wrong.

This check can be carried out on a line-by-line basis if a price look-up electronic register is used.

Unfortunately, this simple control check does not work for food because so many commodities are used in a large number of different dishes. This is not the case with a bottle of beer or a bottle of wine. Some modification may have to be made if the bar has a large cocktails menu. In some ways this resembles the food menu.

LIQUOR PROFIT POTENTIAL
FOR PERIOD   DATE   TO
NUMBER OF DAYS:

COMMODITY	CONSUMPTION		GP% PROFIT	COST OF SALES	% SALE OF TOTAL	STOCK HELD £	STOCK HELD (DAYS)
	COST	SELLING					
SPIRITS	59	220	73.2	26.8	8.7	74	35
APERITIFS	4	12	66.7	33.3	.5	42	300
LIQUEURS	2	8	75.0	25.0	.3	23	328
MINERALS	39	244	84.1	15.9	9.7	36	26
DRAUGHT BEERS	164	550	70.2	21.8	21.8	99	17
BOTTLED BEERS	81	264	69.3	30.7	10.5	53	18
WINES	432	1225	64.7	35.3	48.0	166	11
TOTAL	781	2523	69.0	31.0	100	457	16

LESS ALLOWANCES		124		
	781	2399	67.4	
CASH TAKEN		2370	66.4	
SURPLUS/DEFICIT		29	(1.0)	

1 All figures exclude VAT

2 Allowances credited at selling price

ALLOWANCES

	at cost price	at selling price
ULLAGE	7.50	25.00
DRINKS FOR STAFF	8.90	29.00
FOR COOKING	24.50	70.00
TOTAL		120.00

....
STOCKTAKER

Part Five

Sales, Marketing and Public Relations

William Bailey

It is not enough to get the business organised – it also needs customers! A new restaurant or wine bar may attract customers out of novelty value but this will not last for long and a catering business does not even have this initial boost.

The job of the sales and marketing effort is to create a demand for the product or service and to sustain and satisfy that demand. A simple definition of the catering product is the food and drink. But this is probably too narrow. A better definition takes in everything which happens to customers while they are on the premises or, in the case of a catering company, everything from initial contact to completed event.

This means that the demeanour and behaviour of staff can be almost as important in customer assessment of the product as the menu and the wine list. In a restaurant the ambience and layout will also be important. The marketing effort must take all these areas into consideration.

Market research (see page 25) should have identified potential demand for the business as well as potential user attitudes to the new service. The next step is to set out a marketing strategy designed to reach these potential users.

The marketing tools available are advertising, public relations, direct mail, merchandising through special offers and events, and direct sales. The choice will depend partly on the target audience, partly on the message to be conveyed and partly on the budget.

Attracting Customers

William Bailey

Attracting customers to a new business must be carefully timed. The pre-launch activity must be calculated to build up interest for just the right amount of time without going off the boil. The pre-launch campaign will probably use all five of the marketing tools listed below. The choice will be determined by:

- The size of the budget
- The size of the audience
- The level of response that can be accommodated.

It is also important to decide whether the campaign is primarily designed to build up awareness of the business, to create an image or to build up initial customers. The answer will affect the brief which is given to outside specialists such as advertising or public relations agencies.

Prior to opening, the promotional message is essentially to do with developing customers' anticipations and stimulating interest. Post-opening promotion should represent a radical change in tone. If the customers have responded to the pre-opening campaign, the big build-up, then post-opening promotion should aim to maintain a continuity of awareness, endorsing and building on the initial customer reaction. Once the restaurant has opened the most valuable form of advertising has begun – word of mouth. Research shows that up to 60 per cent of restaurant customers are influenced by recommendation.

Now is the time to develop ongoing interest and excitement about the restaurant in the form of special monthly events, Sunday lunch specials, food festivals and promotions for off-peak periods (see page 179).

Advertising

This is the best means of communicating with the widest potential audience at the cheapest cost per person. But the cost in real terms can be quite high and it may be necessary to run a series of advertisements to get the message over.

is advisable to use a professional advertising agency when planning a major campaign though this is not necessary for a limited campaign in a small locality. An outline brief (see below) can be given to the advertising department of the local paper or radio station which will then prepare the finished advertisement. If the message is clear and you are offering good value this form of advertising can work very well.

With a larger national campaign an advertising agency will advise on the media mix and handle all aspects of design and print buying. Typically, agencies are retained on a monthly fee contract basis. Media commission, the commission the media pays agencies for business placed, should be rebated to the customer. All production charges and bought-in services are charged back to the client subject to an agency commission of 17.65 per cent. Be careful not to spend all the budget on fees rather than the actual campaign.

Whatever the size of the campaign the tone of the advertisement says a great deal about the product you are offering. Try to think of factors which will differentiate the new business from existing ones. The approach may be straightforward and to the point: 'The best value set lunch in town.' 'No fuss, no frills, meet over lunch in one hour flat.' Alternatively, the style may be more obscure. It may try to create the impression that 'This is not just an ordinary restaurant.' 'This is an "in" place.' Whatever approach is chosen it is important to keep the message simple and not try to cover two or three topics in one advertisement.

There are also certain key messages which must be included in an advertisement:

- The name of the restaurant or catering company
- Whether the business is part of a national chain
- The address, telephone and fax numbers
- What is on offer – restaurant, catering facilities, leisure club
- Opening hours, if licensed
- The style of food and drink on offer
- Special features such as jazz on Sundays
- Who to contact for what.

A written brief avoids mistakes and leaves nothing to chance. It should cover the following:

- The objectives of the advertisement
- The main message
- The target customer
- The use of colour or mono
- The media to be used to reach that target
- The timing of the advertisement
- The budget.

Media choice: There is tremendous media choice nowadays. It takes in TV, national and local newspapers, magazines and colour supplements, static poster sites, mobiles (buses and taxis), radio and cinema, sponsorships, local club and charity brochures and many more.

Copy dates vary from a few days for mono advertisements in local papers to 18 weeks for a TV commercial. Production time also varies enormously. Mono advertisements can be created in a few hours. Colour advertisements requiring complex photo shoots can take many weeks and TV commercials many months. Immediacy, budget and the target audience will dictate the choice.

If you are organising your own local campaign you will need to be aware of the advertising production cycle. This requires that you progress and review the various stages in the preparation of the advertisement.

1. Advertising brief
2. Production of visual and draft copy
3. Review and amend
4. Revised visual and copy
5. Approval and minor amendments
6. Artwork
7. Artwork amendment (minimal)
8. Revised artwork
9. Artwork approved and to publication.

Avoid changes at artwork stage as they incur additional costs. When producing colour adverts, a colour proof is produced after artwork. This stage acts as a check on the accuracy of the colour elements only. Layout and copy changes at this stage are expensive.

Special offers and events

The UK catering market is recognised as being one of the most stereotyped in Europe. Little has changed over the last 30 years. The most popular dishes are still prawn cocktail, soup or avocado to start, chicken, peas and chips or steak and chips to follow. The key to retaining trade is to build choice around these eternal favourites.

Every restaurant has to develop its regular and fairly regular diners. This is the audience at whom special offers should be targeted. Word of mouth will build the extra custom. The regular user is keen to try the 'special' and may well invite friends along. The customer who has never visited your restaurant is not going to make his choice because you are running a special promotion for pigs trotters. He will be making his decision based on your mainstream menu.

Events in the calendar and seasonal dishes represent an opportunity to add variety to the basic menu, create a reputation for excitement and fun, and let the customer know that the restaurant or catering business is interested in his custom.

Ideas include:

*   A regular Dish of the Day
*   Menus featuring produce such as fresh asparagus and strawberries in season
*   The arrival of Beaujolais Nouveau or an offer on black velvet cocktails

- Mothers' Day and St Valentine's Day menus and Easter Bunny menus for the children
- Culinary festivals and culture weeks with guest chefs
- Fashion and art festivals with the local arts college
- Open days and recruitment days with local schools and colleges.

Public relations

PR is concerned with building, maintaining and, if necessary, repairing the reputation of the business. Positive stories in the editorial section of the local media, for example, help to make the business into one which local people feel they should use. They can also help to make sure that people know about the promotional events which are planned. Interaction with your market via the editorial pages and programmes of the media is a good deal cheaper than advertising, and the resulting stories are often seen by customers as an endorsement of the business.

Large businesses may hire specialist public relations agencies but most small businesses run their own PR. Start by establishing points of contact. Most editors have too many stories to publish and personal contact can swing the choice your way. Get to know the specialist writers, only send out stories when you really have something to say and be ready to react with a quote on relevant topics of the day. Invite journalists to the restaurant with their partners, not just when you are quiet, but also on busy weekends.

There are a number of PR activities which can be used in an orchestrated programme before, at and after the launch.

Before the launch:

- Announcement of planning consent
- Appointment of architects and designers
- Cutting the first sod
- Foundation stone and topping out ceremony
- Appointment of key staff
- Launch party and press launch.

Once the establishment is open:

- Announcement of special promotions
- Write up on visiting chefs
- Publication of a diary of special events
- Monthly newsletter.

All these activities represent news to the local media and to get the most out of them you need to send out news releases. These are quite easy to write. Stick to the facts and resist the temptation to pad things out. The easier you make it for journalists to write their piece, the more likely they are to use your material. The following checklist will help to ensure that the right information is included.

- A short headline encapsulating the subject of the story
- An introductory paragraph setting out the main elements of who, what, why, where and when
- Three or four further paragraphs developing these elements in order of importance
- If appropriate, include a quotable quote from the 'personality' in charge
- Contact name, address and telephone number for further information.

The contact name and number are arguably the most important items on the whole sheet. They are too often forgotten.

The press release can be accompanied by some ancillary information which may enable you to get two bites of the cherry. These might include background notes on the business, the history of the building, some notable events catered for in the past, black and white photographs of the chef, the manager or the staff at work.

Of course, publicity can come in two forms: good and bad, and whoever is in charge of PR must be prepared for all eventualities. Planning for a calamity or a disaster is essential. The minute a story on fire or food poisoning breaks the media will want a quote. Pre-planning can ensure that the damage is minimised and the reputation of the business protected.

Direct mail

Most experts agree that direct mail is the most cost-effective way of communicating with a target audience. Lists can be bought in or businesses can build up a data base of users by running a business card draw.

Once again, brevity is the key. The recipient of a direct mailshot does not want to read long eulogies on the company. Details of the service you have to offer, perhaps with the endorsement of a few satisfied customers, will do the job very well.

Direct sales

Even though the catering industry tends not to employ vast armies of sales people to prospect for new business, salesmanship is a key element of the work of a restaurateur or caterer. The large majority of buyers will be individuals and the selling role here is mainly to do with direct contact with the client after he has responded to word of mouth recommendation, advertising or PR, and arrived at the restaurant or rung the catering company.

Selling in the restaurant is covered on page 185. Selling in the catering company starts with the telephonist or receptionist who takes the initial enquiry and continues through all contact with the prospective client until the details of a sale are agreed (see below).

The outside caterer, in particular, may also be concerned to attract corporate clients who are unlikely to be influenced by advertising or local public relations activities. Personal sales contact, reputations and sampling the product will count for much more.

Corporate business opportunities include:

- Corporate hospitality organisers such as public relations managers, personnel managers, personal assistants and senior secretaries
- Travel agents and coach and tour operators dealing with both foreign visitors and UK tourists
- Associations and societies organising regular meetings for members
- Conference and exhibition organisers.

All the attributes of good salesmanship will come into play in developing these potential areas. The sales person must be properly trained in presentation, carefully groomed, be out-going and positive, be sensitive to mood. Product knowledge must be balanced with charm, authority and attentiveness in order to develop the confidence of the client.

Types of selling

There are various types of selling and different situations require a different approach.

- *Prospect selling.* This is the pioneering of new accounts by cold canvassing to develop future products and sales.
- *Speciality selling.* Potential customers are selectively researched, targeted and the sales closed by the same person. This method of selling is used for contract accounts.

Sales plans and techniques

The key to effective selling is organisation, planning and timing.

First, the sales person will have a well-defined sales plan taking in the following elements:

- What is to be sold?
- To whom is it to be sold?
- What is the price?
- What is the benefit over the competition?

The plan must be backed up with good product knowledge and an effective presenter.

Second, calls must be timed carefully and not overrun. Punctuality is most important. Follow-up is equally important, particularly after prospect calls. Selling a catering service is very different from selling tangible goods where the product can be sampled at once and an order placed there and then. Often with a service you are competing with an existing supplier and the client has to be persuaded to switch allegiance before he samples.

Learning how to overcome objections is vital and great skill is required to convince the client that there is little risk in switching. Here use can be made of introductory offers or frequent dinner discounts such as two for one. Outside caterers could invite prospective customers to come to hospitality days designed to show off their expertise. In addition to promotional offers, a small presentation pack should be left with the prospective client.

Dealing with Customers and Complaints

William Bailey

Often there is little to choose between competing catering businesses. The menus are all interesting, the decor attractive and the staff efficient at their jobs. But it is the attitude of those staff which can tip the balance so that customers start to choose one outfit rather than another.

It is important to train staff to be friendly and sympathetic to all customers whether they want to spend half the day over lunch or get through their meal in record time. It is often the performance of the staff which can make or break an eating experience by their manner, attitude and approach. For catering companies it is the response to the initial enquiry which can be critical.

Customer relations skills are everything to do with how the customer is addressed and treated by the staff. In a restaurant this includes:

- When a reservation is made by the customer
- When the customer is greeted on arrival at the restaurant
- During the meal
- When the customer leaves.

And in a catering company when:

- An initial enquiry is made by a prospective customer
- Follow-up calls are made to the customer
- The customer is visited for the first time
- The event is taking place
- The event is over.

The relevant staff should be trained how to answer the phone in the correct manner and know what to say and how to say it. They should be briefed about the likely questions they may be asked and how to answer them.

In the restaurant staff need to know how to be attentive without being overbearing, when and how to open up a conversation and when not to, and the best response to questions which are likely to be asked in the restaurant. They should be taught the degree of familiarity that is permitted and when to draw the line.

As well as being the best ambassadors for a catering business, staff can also be the best sales people. Customers are already in a purchasing mood when they enter a restaurant or book a private function and there is profit to be made from extra purchases.

It is well worth the effort of training serving staff to sell. Skilled waiters or barmen can persuade customers to spend just a little more in a low key manner by making helpful suggestions that will both enhance the customers' experience of the restaurant and increase their spend.

The skill is to be pro-active and not re-active to the customers' requirements. It is possible to sum up customers fairly accurately once they have sat down and started to talk. The best approach is to suggest extra accompaniments such as garlic bread, a side salad, a sweet course or cheese even if they are not requested.

On the drinks front ideas include the offer of a bottled mineral water, an aperitif, a half bottle of wine with the starter and a full bottle of wine with the main course or a dessert wine, brandy or liqueur.

Whatever is offered it is important not to be too pushy or to oversell as not only may the extra sale be lost but the customers may not come back again, resulting in a major loss of revenue.

Complaints

It is inevitable that things will sometimes go wrong and a customer has a genuine cause for complaint. No one likes being criticised and taking a complaint personally can create further problems.

'Recognising' and 'owning' the problem are the two key attitudes which must be developed. Customers hate being fobbed off. So the sooner someone takes responsibility for the problem the better. The issue can then be defused and dealt with in a much calmer frame of mind.

Each operation should have an agreed policy regarding customer complaints and comments. It should cover:

- Who deals with complaints and what are the authorities and responsibilities? Does the waiter solve the problem or is it automatically referred to someone more senior?
- What are the agreed remedies if there is a foreign body in the food, if the food is cold or if the food is actually OK? Should all plates be cleared and a fresh start made or is it just the offending plate which is removed? Should the waiter say nothing and replace it or is there a set response?
- What is the overall attitude to complaints? Staff must know what is in the owner's mind. Is the customer always right? Is the customer sometimes right or is the customer always wrong!

The adage is that 'The customer is always right', but 'sometimes right' may be more accurate. There are usually two sides to the story and it is always necessary to obtain the facts, particularly where there is a question of refunds. Irate customers have fertile imaginations and the truth is often less dramatic than their account of the incident.

It is important that all staff know how to deal with complaints. Here is a checklist for dealing with them:

- Acknowledge the customer's complaint at once
- Ensure the location is right to handle the complaint
- Defuse the irate customer with an offer of help
- Make written notes on a formal report form
- Resist the temptation automatically to agree with everything the customer says
- If at all possible the customer should be satisfied before he or she leaves but it may be necessary to ask for time to obtain further information, perhaps from an off-duty member of staff
- Whatever the outcome thank the customer for having drawn the matter to your attention.

Recording complaints and suggestions is a good idea so that longer-term trends in customer satisfaction can be monitored and the improvement rate reviewed from time to time with staff at staff meetings.

Keeping Standards Up and Monitoring

William Bailey

The reputation of a restaurant or catering business is essentially a combination of static measurements by a third party such as a guide book and variable measurements in the form of customer recommendation. Both are the result of the ability consistently to deliver the expected quality in terms of value for money, standard of food and wine and customer service. They both offer a measure of how standards are being maintained.

The difference between the two is that the business can continuously improve its reputation with customers on a day-to-day basis but once it has been graded by a guide it is stuck with that grade, good or bad, for a year.

High standards must not only be attained to attract customers, they must also be maintained to keep customers. It is easy to let things slip when the business is stretched or complacency sets in. The answer is to monitor performance on a regular basis.

This can be done on the spot by assessing staff performance and on paper by a regular scrutiny of the sales records. Independent outside assessors can also be retained to visit the establishment or arrange small catered events incognito. Customer questionnaires are another useful form of outside assessment.

Part Six

Personnel Management

Chris Ripper

In any catering business staffing usually forms the largest variable cost on the business. It is important both to get the staffing levels right and to develop a core of loyal and hard-working employees who are well trained and well motivated. The personnel manager's job takes in the recruitment and selection of staff, employment contracts, grievance procedures and trade union contact as well as the training, development and motivation of staff.

Hours of Work

Chris Ripper

In considering staffing requirements, the goal must always be to match the available staff hours of work to the business requirements; no more and no less. In practice, staffing requirements will change according to the department, time of day, day of the week and seasonally. The main points to consider are outlined below.

Forecast

An accurate daily/weekly forecast of required staff hours in each department is necessary for effective staff control. It may be useful here to employ work standards such as the number of covers served per hour per employee. The forecast must look sufficiently far ahead to allow time for adjustment to work hours and notification.

Contracted hours

A balance needs to be struck between a core of full-time staff contracted for 39 hours per week, which is a fixed cost on the business, and part-time staff contracted for a minimum number of hours per week but available to work additional hours when required. When recruiting, contract the minimum number of hours per week but indicate to the applicant the average hours that the individual may expect to work. In this way the ability to flex hours from week to week is retained, but the individual has an indication of the average hours and therefore the average weekly wage.

Switching staff from one department to another according to demand helps to reduce cost and can provide additional job interest. Points to consider include training requirements and the need for good inter-departmental communication and cooperation. Job rotation generally operates well in smaller establishments but becomes more difficult to coordinate in larger establishments.

Rotas and overtime

Weekly work rotas should be as flexible as possible. Start and finish times may not be the same for each day of the week as demand patterns can vary; so too should staff hours.

Avoid setting weekly work rotas for staff that go further ahead than the ability to forecast business accurately and therefore staffing requirements. Try to avoid providing the same days off each week where this inhibits ability to match staffing requirements to business forecast.

Split shifts are a traditional way of reducing staff costs but in today's climate split shifts have drawbacks in terms of acceptability and should be avoided.

Overtime is normally payable only after 39 hours worked in a week. Various premium arrangements may apply. As a guide, time and a half for the sixth day of work and double time for the seventh day are common. Work on a public holiday normally carries double time plus a day off in lieu.

Agreement may be reached to offer time off in lieu of overtime with a proviso that time off be taken within a fixed period (say 30 days) following the overtime being incurred.

As far as possible, allocate time off for holidays during quieter business periods. Prepare a chart for the year ahead showing how many staff in each department may take holiday in any one week. Prioritising these weeks can be done on a first come, first served basis or, alternatively, priority may be given to longer serving staff or staff looking for time off during school holidays because of family commitments.

Casual staff

Casual staff work as required. They are not employees and do not hold a contract of employment. However, the customer will not know the difference. It is therefore important that casuals are trained and motivated in the same way as employees. This will also help to build up a brigade of loyal casuals readily available as required. It is useful in establishing this relationship to provide casuals with an agreement setting out the basis on which work is offered.

Sample Banqueting/Casual Worker Agreement

Nature of engagement

The basis of your engagement is that you are not regarded as an employee of the company by working under a contract of employment.

Work will be offered to you on an *ad hoc* basis as and when there is work to be done. You are free to accept or decline such offers of work. You are not guaranteed continuous engagement and the company is under no obligation to offer you further engagements or re-engagement. This statement does not therefore constitute a contract of employment between you and the company.

Engagements will be offered to you on either an hourly or sessional basis. Attendance at work will be as agreed between yourself and the hotel manager or his representative. When you have agreed to attend for work and are unable to do so, you are required to notify the hotel immediately.

No sick pay benefit applies to your engagement in the event that you are unable to attend work because of sickness or injury.

Wages
You will be paid in arrears and National Insurance contributions and income tax payments, at the appropriate rate, will be deducted if applicable.

Holiday pay
You will not receive payment in respect of holidays regardless of the number of engagements and hours worked by you.

Health and safety at work
Under the Health and Safety at Work Act each individual has a legal responsibility for their own welfare and for the health and safety of others. Specific instructions relating to the operation of machinery etc are displayed at or near the relevant place of work. Any queries you may have relating to health and safety matters should be raised in the first instance with the person to whom you are immediately responsible.

Code of conduct
During each individual engagement, as defined on the new start form, you will be subject to the company's standards of conduct and departmental rules. You are responsible for maintaining high standards of work and personal behaviour and conduct. Your immediate supervisor has the authority to suspend or terminate your engagement prior to the conclusion of the agreed period should there be a breach on your part of the relevant standards of conduct or behaviour.

Acknowledgement
Name ....

I acknowledge receipt and acceptance of the terms of engagement as set out above

Signed.. Date...

Recruitment and Selection

Chris Ripper

Careful recruitment and selection is the first step towards building a stable and well-trained workforce. The following guidelines may be useful.

Sources of staff

There are a number of different ways of making contact with potential job candidates. Which one is chosen will depend on the position to be filled and the cost. Choices include:

Advertising: Advertising includes the use of local or trade press. Lineage advertisements are the cheapest followed by semi-display and display advertisements. While the newspaper or journal will set advertisements, the use of a specialist agency will guarantee a more professional job. Other possibilities include use of shop windows, leaflet drops and leaflet inserts into free circulation newspapers.

Recruitment agencies: These agencies exist to provide a recruitment service. Use an agency that specialises in the relevant job market. Most will charge a negotiable fee between 10 and 20 per cent of annual salary on placement. Check to ensure that there is a satisfactory rebate should the candidate who is placed leave within the first six months. Agencies work most effectively if they are carefully briefed as to the position to be filled and the type of candidate required.

Recruitment forums: These are normally organised as open days within the establishment. The forum provides an opportunity to display and demonstrate various aspects of employment and to process a relatively large number of people through the selection procedure. It is a shop window for the establishment to potential candidates. It should be planned and managed professionally.

Personal recommendation: New staff joining the organisation often know others who may be interested in job opportunities. Further stimulation can be provided via a recruitment bonus. Normally this works on the basis that existing members of staff are rewarded for recruiting new staff subject to that individual remaining in employment for a minimum period, normally three to six months.

Job/personal descriptions

These documents need not be unduly complicated. They serve a useful purpose for the following reasons:

- Preparation of job descriptions and person specifications makes the person responsible for recruitment think about the job and the skills required to fill that job.
- Documents may be used to brief agencies preparing advertising material or searching for candidates on behalf of the organisation.
- A person specification may be used when interviewing as a check against the skills of the candidates.
- Demonstrates to candidates a thorough and professional approach to the interview process. If the organisation is in competition for staff, such professionalism may swing the balance between acceptance and rejection of a job offer.

Sample Job Description

Job title: Waiter/Waitress

Responsible to: Head waiter

Main objective: To provide an efficient and friendly service of food and drink to all customers

Specific responsibilities
1. To take full responsibility for the efficient provision of food service for a designated number of tables (a station).
2. To acknowledge and welcome customers brought to the station.
3. To offer drinks and make helpful suggestions.
4. To provide menus and highlight any house specials, or other useful information, to help the customer's choice.
5. To take orders using the opportunity to suggest additional items, where appropriate to up-sell.
6. To progress the order through the kitchen.
7. To deliver food to the table, wishing the customer an enjoyable meal.
8. To check that all is to the customer's satisfaction, and report all guests' comments to the management.
9. To clear and take further orders, as appropriate, when the customer is ready.
10. To provide the bill and take payment, thanking the customer for their patronage.
11. To prepare the station ready for service before the commencement of each shift, and clear and tidy the station at the end of each shift.

12. To carry out delegated tasks to prepare the restaurant for service and clear down at the end of service.
13. To maintain at all times specified standards of personal and food hygiene.
14. To handle all money for the guest's account in accordance with the instructions from the management.
15. To ensure the safekeeping of bills and use in accordance with instructions given.

Terms and conditions

Pay: £ per hour, payable weekly by credit transfer to a bank or building society.

Hours: A minimum of three evening sessions per week 6.00 pm–11.00 pm.

During busy times of the year, additional shifts would be available.

Holidays: Twelve days' paid holiday per annum pro rata to service in the calendar year. Holidays may be taken by prior arrangement.

Uniform: Two shirts/blouses plus one trousers/skirt are provided.

Meals on duty: Where a shift is in excess of four hours, a meal is provided.

Discount: Employees and up to three guests may eat at a discount of 25 per cent at any company restaurant.

Transport: If public transport is not available at the end of the shift, an account taxi will be provided.

Sample Person Specification

Job title: Waiter/Waitress

Education: No specific requirements. Ideally City and Guilds or NVQ Level 2 in Food Service. Able to converse in satisfactory English

Experience: Evidence of successful employment involving provision of face-to-face service to customers

Health: Able to work standing for long periods

Domestic: Able to work evenings and weekends

Application forms and references

The easiest way to gather basic information concerning applicants is to ask for completion of a simple application form. Do not fall into the trap of asking for a CV and then sending an application form. This merely provides duplicate information and probably annoys the prospective candidate. In some ways, application forms are better than CVs because they should contain all the information required set out in the same way for each candidate.

References can provide a good guide to performance with previous employers. Open references are provided by ex-employers to an individual usually at the time of termination of employment. They do have some value but bear in mind that in general they will refer only to the strengths of the individual.

Take up written or verbal references with past employers. A written reference will normally confirm dates of employment and provide basic information concerning competence. Sometimes, replies to requests for written references may be rather bland and a telephone call may elicit more explicit information.

Planning and running the interview

Proper planning of the interview process will assist in providing a professional interview and in making the right selection decision. Good planning should include the following features:

- Arrange the time for the interview in a comfortable environment where disturbance is unlikely.
- Notify the candidate of the interview time and try to stick to it.
- Provide details of how to get to the unit location.
- Read the application form thoroughly and make a note of any questions to be asked.
- Identify questions which are likely to provide information on the skills which a candidate has and his or her ability to put those skills into practice.
- Consider whether a practical test may be of value. In its simplest form this could include laying and clearing a table in a restaurant or preparing a dish.
- More sophisticated tests are available which assess such attributes as verbal ability, numerical ability and even personality. However, such tests almost invariably require a trained administrator and interpreter. No test does any more than add to the available information about the candidate.
- Have to hand a job description to discuss with the candidate.
- Have to hand a list of the terms and conditions associated with the job.

The purpose of the interview is, first, to obtain sufficient information to make a decision as to whether the candidate matches the job requirements and, second, to provide the candidate with sufficient information to make a decision as to whether the position is of interest. The following pointers will help:

- Try to relax the candidate (and yourself) with a minute or two of small talk.
- Indicate the way in which the interview is to be conducted. A useful guide here is to follow the layout of the application form.
- Try to ask open-ended questions that demand information or opinion rather than a yes/no answer.
- Listen 80 per cent of the time and talk 20 per cent.
- Look for evidence of achievement. To help, it is quite legitimate to pose hypothetical situations and ask candidates what course of action they might adopt.
- Check such obvious areas as health and availability to work the hours required.
- Prepare and provide information to the candidate concerning the organisation, the job, and the terms and conditions of employment.
- Give a clear indication as to when the candidate may expect to hear the outcome of the interview.

- Evaluate the information gained against the person specification and make brief notes after the interview. Don't leave it too long because, after several interviews, your recollection of particular individuals may fade.

Discrimination

It is illegal to discriminate against any individual at work on grounds of race, colour, sex or ethnic origin. Furthermore, any individual applying for a job has a statutory right to seek redress should he or she believe that discrimination has taken place at any stage in the selection procedure. An open mind, free of prejudice, is essential if both the letter and the spirit of the law are to be met. In the event that a discrimination claim is brought against the organisation, it will be necessary to demonstrate that the selection process was conducted without prejudice. It may also be necessary to produce evidence in support of decisions made concerning the suitability or otherwise of candidates having regard to the job description and the person specification.

Terms and Conditions

Chris Ripper

Every employee is entitled to receive a contract or written particulars of employment within two calendar months of the commencement of employment. The written particulars of employment or documents referred to therein must include the following specific information:

- The names of the employer and the employee
- The job title of the employee
- The place of work
- The date of commencement of employment plus the date of commencement of any previous but continuous employment with the company
- The rate of pay
- The intervals at which payments are made
- The method of calculation of premium payments
- Conditions relating to working hours
- Calculation of paid holiday entitlement, including public holidays
- Pension scheme provisions
- Details of any collective agreements in force
- Expected duration of work if not permanent
- Sickness benefit entitlement
- The disciplinary and grievance procedures
- Length of notice of termination of employment by either party.

Written notification of changes to the above must be given within one month of the change taking place.

It is normal practice for both employer and employee to sign copies of the written particulars.

Pay and gratuities

The following factors should be considered when determining the rate of pay:

- Pay may be specified per hour, per week or per annum. Clearly where hours are flexible or there is entitlement to premium payments, it is easier to work with an hourly rate.
- The level of pay may be determined by local market rates. The relevant trade associations can often help with pay survey information.
- Ensure that the pay differentials with other managers and staff take due account of levels of responsibility as well as providing attractive opportunity for career progression.
- Consider additional pay increments for additional skills.
- Pay can be directly related to work done. However, it is important to strike a balance between reward for speed of completion and maintenance of quality standards.
- There is a statutory obligation to provide a payslip at the end of each pay period showing total pay, monies deducted and net pay.
- No deduction may be made from an employee's pay other than statutory deductions unless the written authority of the employee has been obtained in advance.

Profit related pay (PRP) is that part of an employee's pay which is formally linked to the profits of the business. Since new legislation in 1988, PRP schemes may be registered with the Inland Revenue. Under a registered PRP scheme, one half of PRP payments may be free of tax up to a prescribed limit.

In order for a PRP scheme to qualify for registration, it has to meet a number of criteria. Full notes for guidance in setting up a PRP scheme are available from the Inland Revenue.

Some businesses make a service charge to the customer indicating that no further gratuities are expected and that the service charge is divided among the staff. Others make no service charge, and indicate that gratuities are at the customer's discretion.

Normally the distribution of tips is determined between staff and individual heads of department. It is wise to ensure that the system of distribution is clearly understood by all concerned and seen to be a fair reflection of effort and responsibility. If there is direct company involvement in the collection and distribution of gratuities, the company is obliged to undertake responsibility for PAYE deductions.

Whatever the system adopted for the distribution of gratuities, it is essential to check with the Inland Revenue concerning tax liability. If the liability for the payment of tax rests with the employee, the employer has an obligation to make this clear to the individuals concerned.

Benefits
Listed below are some of the options for consideration:

- The provision of pay to individuals who are off sick. The duration of sickness pay and the level is normally determined by the individual's hours of work and service. Payment while off sick is normally net of statutory sick pay entitlements.

- Paid holiday days per annum. Holiday pay is normally accrued during the holiday year. For example, two days' holiday pay for every five weeks worked in the calendar year up to a maximum of 20 days after 50 weeks. In some organisations, holiday pay is accrued in the current year for payment in the following year though this practice is less common today.
- Provision of uniforms
- Provision of private health insurance
- Provision of discounts on in-house purchases of goods or services
- Provision of discount facilities negotiated with local retail/leisure businesses
- Provision of free or subsidised meals on duty
- Provision of live-in accommodation
- Provision of pension and/or life assurance.

Some of the benefits listed above may be taxable and advice should be sought from the Inland Revenue.

Incentives

Incentives are used to recognise and reward performance. Incentive schemes designed to provide recognition may be classified as high value/low cost schemes. Typical examples include employee of the month/year, long service awards and competitions on sales achievement. An example of the latter might be a small prize for the individual who sells most of a particular product over a short period.

More sophisticated incentive schemes provide pay linked to performance. Such schemes must be simple and easy to understand. They must also be seen to be fair and the targets achievable. A maximum incentive payment should be specified. Remember that the shorter the period over which payment may be earned, the greater the motivation. It should be made clear that an incentive scheme is not part of the terms and conditions of employment and is subject to review.

Disciplinary and Grievance Procedures

Chris Ripper

These procedures are a necessary feature of the formal relationship between the employer and the employee. The procedures provide a vehicle for the employee to raise formally any areas of concern and for the employer to bring to the attention of the employee matters relating to that individual's conduct or performance. When used properly, both procedures make for a better understanding between employer and employee.

The Advisory Conciliation and Arbitration Service (ACAS) publishes an advisory handbook entitled *Discipline at Work* which provides detailed guidance on the development and operation of a disciplinary procedure.

The handbook does not specifically cover the construction and operation of a grievance or appeal procedure. However, exactly the same principles apply as for a disciplinary procedure. The employee, via the procedure, is given a hearing at which to air a grievance or set out an appeal. Furthermore, that procedure provides for a further hearing at a more senior level in the event that the employee is not satisfied with the response at the first hearing.

6.5

Trade Unions

Chris Ripper

Any employee has a statutory right to belong or not to belong to a trade union of his or her choice.

An organisation may be approached to enter into an agreement with a trade union which has significant membership within that organisation. Such an agreement may provide representation rights such that the employees in membership may be represented by the trade union in a disciplinary or grievance procedure. The agreement may be extended to include negotiating rights on matters relating to pay and conditions. Most trade unions today seek to work with employers to the mutual benefit of the organisation and the employees.

6.6

Training and Development

Chris Ripper

Effective training within an organisation provides far and away the best opportunity to influence the attitude and performance of employees.

The involvement of all line management in the training process is essential to effective training. Some managers will try to avoid this responsibility because of lack of confidence and experience. However, given support and training, nearly all line managers enjoy training and the opportunity which it provides for them to pass on their professional knowledge and skills in a structured way.

Areas to be considered when creating training programmes include the following: induction, fire, food hygiene, control of substances hazardous to health (COSHH), manual handling, first aid, technical skills, product knowledge, customer service. In many of these areas, there is a 'statutory requirement' to carry out training.

Effective training starts with a clear understanding of the knowledge or skills that trainees will acquire and be able to demonstrate as a result of the training. The next step is to develop a training plan setting out how these skills and knowledge are to be transferred to the trainee.

Trainees will always learn best when given the opportunity to discuss the issues taught and obtain practical hands-on experience. Accordingly, training sessions should be planned to encourage dialogue rather than monologue and to include, where possible, the use of practical exercises.

Here are some examples of training ideas which may be used to make training memorable:

- Improve product knowledge through tasting or even blind tasting
- Use quiz games to test understanding, perhaps with a small prize
- Check out the local competition with trainees then use the training session to identify lessons to be learned

- Use trainees to demonstrate acquired skills to the group
- Provide work-based projects which require the trainee to seek out knowledge or information
- Provide relevant reading materials before or after the training session
- Consider the use of relevant training videos
- Set up employee/customer role plays replicating real-life scenarios.

It is important that training is evaluated in order to determine whether the required standard has been achieved. This can be done in the form of an on-the-job assessment or by the use of tests or quizzes. Trainees will generally feel that training has been more worthwhile if their progress is measured, competence assessed and the results discussed with them.

On completion of training, provide some high value/low cost recognition – perhaps a training certificate appropriately worded and signed or a small prize for the best achievement against the training objectives.

Consider how best to instigate a follow-up system after training to ensure that the lessons learned are put into practice with good effect.

Motivation

Chris Ripper

Employees spend long periods of time in the workplace. The wrong atmosphere can give rise to loss of job interest, demotivation and, ultimately, poor performance. The following pointers should be considered when addressing this issue:

- Routine is important to many employees who value knowing exactly what is required of them. However, some may be motivated by increased opportunity for decision-making. Consider whether there are aspects of each job which may be placed more specifically under the authority of the job holder.
- When taking decisions about the business, managers should ask the opinions of the relevant employees. Opinion-seeking provides recognition to the employee and may often result in worthwhile input. It can also encourage support for a decision when taken.
- Individual recognition, be it a simple daily greeting or considered praise, goes a long way. Conversely, its absence is invariably noticed.
- Determine what information is really confidential. In practice, much that is held to be confidential is actually nothing of the kind. Employees will develop a sense of pride and involvement through being made aware of business results, forecasts and plans.
- Evaluate the effectiveness of existing communication channels. Walk the job and ask employees if they have received communicated information.
- Review the working environment. Poor staff facilities encourage poor standards in the workplace.
- Employees will benefit from a formal review of performance against agreed objectives on a regular basis. As a separate exercise, a review of training and development needs and career aspirations, together with an action plan for the future, is desirable.

Part Seven

Property Maintenance and Waste Management

Brian Ridgway

Property may be the company's main asset, if not the only asset. It is therefore important that it is maintained and managed properly. It must be capable of housing the business efficiently and, if at all possible, it should not be allowed to decline in value.

What is done and how will depend upon a number of factors such as:

- The size of the property
- The construction of the property
- The general condition of the property
- The function of the property
- The condition of the plumbing, the gas, the electrical and mechanical equipment, the paintwork, decorations, drains and fabrics
- The size and scope of the business now, and in the foreseeable future
- Any immediate alterations or new equipment to be purchased
- The proximity of the property to others
- Possible noise problems in residential areas, from late-night restaurants or night-time production kitchens
- Legal constraints
- The practical and theoretical knowledge of the management team.

Maintenance Plan

Brian Ridgway

Maintenance management should be pro-active. There is no sense in waiting until a breakdown occurs. This simply causes havoc. Set up a maintenance plan as soon as the business is up and running.

The plan must address the following questions:

- Which aspects of the property need regular maintenance?
- To what standard will they be maintained?
- How frequently must maintenance work be carried out?
- How much can be done by unskilled workers and how much will require specific skills?
- Is there expertise within the operation which could be used in some areas and if so, who and where?
- Will full-time or part-time help be required?
- Would a contract with an outside company to service all areas on a regular basis together with a call-out facility be a suitable option?

The plan must also take into account capital planning so that improvements, renovations and expansions can be brought on line to take advantage of opportunities as they present themselves.

Start the plan by taking stock of the whole property and make a record of the condition of each aspect. The plan should detail the work likely to be carried out during the coming year together with a budget cost figure which may or may not be the actual figure at the time.

This should obviously be done at the same time as the budget or business plan. The plan should then be reassessed by a similar stock taking every six months. In the event the equipment may last longer than envisaged or the paintwork may be improved to the required standard by washing rather than by painting.

Specialists

In most cases simple day-to-day maintenance such as the changing of light bulbs and repair to paintwork and furniture can be carried out by the management or employees but the more technical work should be carried out by specialists. Anything requiring a certificate should be carried out by a professionally qualified technician.

Items which require qualified specialists include: lifts and hoists, boilers, ovens, air-conditioning systems, refrigerators, washing machines, extractor fans, pumps, cooling towers, ventilation and water systems, fire alarms and electrical protection equipment and sprinkler systems.

Timing

These areas need to be serviced either according to the manufacturer's instructions or at sensible frequencies based on experience. The idea is not to service too frequently, thereby causing unnecessary expenditure, or too infrequently, thereby putting the business at risk. If the worst happens, infrequent servicing will cause unnecessary panic expenditure which is always more costly.

Although there may be a range of service intervals it is sensible to group as many as possible together, so that a contracting company can carry out a number of services at the same time. This also acts as an *aide-mémoire* to those responsible that a number of items need servicing.

The specific timing of refurbishment, improvement and the installation of equipment needs careful thought. Night work may seem to be a big extra expense but shutting the restaurant may prove costlier. Shutting the restaurant for half days at a time when the lunch business is poor may be an even better answer, or it might be best to pick the two worst weeks of the year to shut the restaurant, send the staff on holiday and do the work. In planned maintenance and property management there are generally a number of alternatives from which to choose.

Energy Management

Brian Ridgway

In its simplest form energy management relates to the careful and prudent use of gas, electricity and water. If the situation is not managed the unrestricted use of these commodities will lead to wasted energy and unnecessary costs being incurred.

Start by choosing the most efficient equipment. By and large gas-fired equipment is cheaper to run than electrical equipment. Whatever the fuel, make sure that you have been informed about the tariffs available and that you are on the most suitable and most economic tariff for your business.

Do not run equipment for longer than is absolutely necessary. Use time clocks to make sure of this. Choose instantly heated hot water boilers (like commercial Ascots) rather than hot water that is stored. This way you only heat what you require.

Do not allow management and staff to turn on all the equipment the moment they arrive at work if it is not going to be required for an hour or two; make sure that all equipment is turned off the moment it is not required.

For example:

- You may not need the extracting equipment while some of the basic preparation is being done.
- The grill chef will not need the grill until just before the restaurant opens.
- Coffee will not be required until the first diners are at the end of their meal.
- Do not overheat the kitchen and restaurant in the winter, only to have to cool it down later on during the service.
- Do not let kitchen staff continuously run hot or cold water when they don't actually need it.
- Do not allow chefs to run gas and electric hobs at a high temperature unless they are required at that temperature.

Finally, check round the premises at the end of each service period to ensure that all equipment and lights have been turned off.

7.3

Waste Management

Brian Ridgway

Waste from business premises is now controlled by law and businesses have a duty of care which means that they must take all reasonable steps to look after waste and prevent its illegal disposal by others. *A Code of Practice: Waste Management – The Duty of Care* is available from HMSO.

The best methods to ensure the safe storage and disposal of waste will depend upon the following factors:

- The type of waste items: food scraps, used fat or oil, cardboard/paper, tins, plastic, bottles, broken glass and china
- The volume of waste in each area
- The frequency and cost of local council services
- The cost of private contractors
- The space available for the handling and storage of waste.

Small businesses will probably use strong plastic sacks which are tied securely and stored until collection. More and more businesses are segregating waste according to type before bagging. The waste can then be recycled when appropriate.

Larger operations may use compactors for all waste apart from bottles. There are a number of types and sizes of compactors ranging from a simple hand-controlled model to a large automatic electrically operated model. Bottles are segregated according to colour and stored in sacks or cardboard boxes.

Care must be taken to ensure that the waste storage area and waste bins, where used, are kept clean and regularly hosed down and scrubbed with detergent and disinfectant, otherwise vermin and flies will be attracted which could then contaminate the kitchen area.

It is also important to check that the person or company collecting the waste is legally authorised to do so. Council waste collectors are obviously registered and there is no need to check further. Other carriers must be registered and this can be confirmed with the local council. The only exceptions to registration are charities and voluntary organisations.

When waste changes hands there is a requirement to complete a transfer note. This note is signed by both parties and is accompanied by a written description of the waste handed over. A model form published by the government is included with the Code of Practice.

The transfer note should include what the waste is, how much there is and what it is packed in; the time, date and place of the transfer; and details of both parties. If collections are carried out on a regular basis only one annual transfer note is required for each contractor.

The description of the waste must provide as much information as someone else might need to handle it safely. Both the description and the transfer note must be kept for two years as they may have to be produced in court.

Part Eight

Security

Brian Mumford

In any business, management has a duty to protect its assets. It also has a duty not to put undue temptation before employees. Magistrates have been known to be lenient or even dismiss charges where there are no security or control systems and discipline is slack.

Security systems are also important because they protect the owners of the business from loss via employees and outside thieves, they also protect innocent employees and customers.

Security of Property Assets

Brian Mumford

Probably the most obvious aspect of property control is an adequate locking system with key control.

Doors and windows

Entrance keys, and this includes front, back and side doors, are normally held by the owner or line manager with spares held by a senior trusted employee. Deposit the name, address and telephone number of the key holders at the local police station in case of emergency or if a burglar alarm is set off. Security lock companies and your insurance company will advise on the types of lock to use.

Internal keys will be required to control store rooms, chillers, fridges and freezers and in a large establishment for internal doors to public areas, different sections of the kitchen and preparation areas, and store rooms.

With internal keys it is a good idea to work on a master-key, sub-master and single-door key system. Electronic digital systems with variable code numbers can also be installed. With the former system the master key is held by the owner/ manager, the sub-master by middle managers, supervisors or heads of department and single-door keys or groupings of single-door keys by more junior employees who are authorised to have access.

The control of spare keys is essential so a record must be made of lost keys and the issue of replacements. Depending on which key has been lost it may be necessary to replace that lock completely or swop it with another one without disclosing to anyone that the transfer has taken place. In all cases limit the number of spare keys.

If combination locks or padlocks are used the combination should be changed about once a month or within a shorter period if it is thought that the combination has been discovered by someone not authorised to gain access.

Windows should not be forgotten when looking at property security. The type of glass and window locks should both be considered.

Alarms and surveillance

If your premises are situated in an area where theft is prevalent, it might be worth considering the installation of intruder or burglar alarms and possibly a closed circuit TV surveillance system. This should include comprehensive video recording with date time logging of incidents. Unless the system is monitored or programmed to record and highlight specific activity, such as movement through a particular door or area, it will not make a viable contribution.

Car park

Restaurant car parks in particular are often targeted by car thieves either to steal the car itself or take articles of value from inside it.

Proprietors should display notices that can be read by all customers or staff using the car park to the effect that cars are parked at the owners' risk and that the proprietor will not accept any responsibility for loss or damage to vehicles or contents.

However, proprietors do have a duty to ensure that customers' property is safeguarded as much as is reasonably possible, and in any case it is in the proprietor's interest to do so or the customers may go elsewhere.

Some areas are worse than others but in those areas where theft is prevalent it makes sense to illuminate the car park, and possibly install a surveillance camera coupled with movement sensors if the instances of theft rise too steeply. Random checks of the car park by staff at busy times are a sensible deterrent.

Cloakrooms

Where coats and bags are accepted by staff from customers for safe keeping, they should be held in a designated secure area. Display a disclaimer notice covering loss or damage to property while in the management's care. Issue numbered receipts and return the property on production of the receipt. If possible, print the disclaimer on the reverse of the ticket.

The cloakroom should either be constantly manned or locked when unattended. Alternatively, a self-help cloakroom system should be available enabling customers to secure their property adequately.

Security of Cash

Brian Mumford

Key control

The main safe should be controlled by more than one key or by combination lock. In larger organisations it is wise to ensure that *two* senior managers have to be present to open the safe, each having one key or one knowing the combination and the other having the key. This is a particularly wise precaution overnight as there have been many instances of owners and senior managers being dragged from their beds to open safes for thieves.

It may also be sensible to place the safe in a room which is also controlled by two keys. The police, safe manufacturers and your insurance company can advise on the procedures most appropriate to your business.

Cash handlers should be the subject of detailed background enquiries to ensure that their track record is sound. Referees should be made aware that the position involves the handling of cash so that they can make appropriate comments.

Birth certificates, passports and records of previous employment should all be checked to ensure that applicants are who they say they are. It is easy to assume a false identity. Fidelity insurance should be considered for management and those handling large amounts of cash or stock.

Keys for cash boxes holding floats or takings must also be controlled so that there is a continuous record of who had the key and therefore access to the money in the box. Too often shortages of cash cannot be traced back to one person because handovers went unrecorded and the contents of the cash box have not been checked when the keys were handed over. Spare keys must be kept separately in a place that cannot be accessed by anyone but the owner/manager. These principles should also be employed for the security of safe keys.

Cash register keys must also be controlled and again a record kept of the holder on an ongoing basis, unless it is always the same manager. Under no circumstances should the till read key or the zero key be given to staff unless you have complete trust in them.

Handling cash

There are a number of steps which can be taken to reduce temptation and make it less easy for dishonest staff to steal cash themselves or help others to do so. These include:

- Use modern cash registers and terminals which, though more expensive, can be programmed to record individual employee activity such as payments in or stock movement. They should require the employee to declare a cash total before the total of the machine transactions for that individual is revealed.
- Milk tills regularly throughout the day and deposit in the main safe or in a letterbox drop facility at the bank.
- Do not bank monies at the same time every day and alter the rota of personnel visiting the bank. If employees go to the bank, always insist on two going together.
- Employ a cash in transit collection service for banking and collection of payroll.
- Install surveillance systems.

Security of Property

Brian Mumford

This applies to customers' and staff property as well as to food, drink and items of equipment.

Prevention of theft

There are a number of steps which should be taken to cut theft to a minimum.

- Never allow deliveries when there is no one to receive them.
- Do not leave goods outside the back door unattended and ensure that delivered goods are not taken off the van and put straight back on again.
- All store rooms, wine cellars, large fridges and freezers should be kept under lock and key and only minimum quantities delivered from store to kitchen.
- Lock up all expensive items and mark with an identity code by stamping or labelling with ultra violet ink.
- Limit the number of people who have access to stores and kitchen and lock up kitchen stores at night.
- Consider routines for issuing keys and authority levels allowed to have access to keys (see pages 217–218 and 219–220).
- Keep proper stock records (see pages 127–128 and 141–142).
- Keep a register of all major and minor items of equipment showing the serial number, the date bought and a short description of the item. From time to time make a check against the register.
- Institute efficient cost control systems and ensure that staff receive regular training in all security matters.
- Watch for staff acting suspiciously (see page 223) and watch for staff eating or drinking the profits away.
- Property belonging to the business should not leave the premises unless it is detailed on an official delivery note or 'pass out' specifically allowing removal of the article.

- From time to time employees leaving the building should be asked to disclose the contents of their carrier bags, handbags and parcels. The object of this kind of spot check, which all employees must be informed might happen at any time, is not so much to catch thieves but to act as a preventive measure which places no one under suspicion. Care must be taken to ensure that it is both random and at the same time involves all employees over a period of time. Keep a record of any checks.

Powers of search

- The powers of a private person to search the property, or the person, of an individual are strictly limited.
- Any unlawful search or retention of property is a trespass and can give rise to a claim for damages.
- There is no power to search lockers or property or the person *except by consent*.
- There is no power to search a person to find out if he or she committed a crime, even if something is found, *except by consent*.
- It seems that a private person upon lawfully arresting a suspected offender may take and detain property found in the offender's possession if the property is likely to afford material evidence for the prosecution in respect of the offence for which the offender has been arrested. Property not connected with the offence should not be taken.
- The fact that a search clause is inserted into the contract of employment of a person does not empower you to enforce a search. A search can only be carried out if the person *agrees* to be searched *at the time*. To compel a search would be assault, and is actionable.
- Males will not search females, under any circumstances, and vice versa.
- Searching should always be done in private.

All kitchen employees should be provided with lockable lockers to store their clothes and female employees should be able to lock up their handbags if they work in an office area. Lockers should be inspected from time to time. Keep a record of any inspections. Make sure that staff know they should not keep items of equipment in their lockers.

Make sure that everyone knows what will happen if they try to misappropriate either company or guests' property (prosecution or dismissal). This includes either taking food and drink off the premises *and* consuming unauthorised items on the premises.

Lost and found property

The most efficient way to manage lost and found property is to keep registers of customers' lost and found property.

Check all property reported lost on the premises against the Found Register and if it is not there record it in the Lost Register. The records should show:

- A description of the article
- The day, date and time it was found

- The location of the find
- The finder's name
- A column to show the date that it was either claimed or disposed of
- A column for the name and address of the claimant.

The finding of valuable property, wallets and bank notes should be reported to the police.

Efforts should be made to restore found property to the rightful owner without delay. It should be stored under lock and key to ensure that it does not 'disappear', particularly if it is an attractive or valuable item.

Never forward property to anyone without ensuring that the claimant is the rightful owner. It is important to make the claimant describe the article first before it is pronounced found.

Property not claimed after a reasonable period of time can be disposed of by giving to charity or selling to raise money for staff funds or returning to the finder. Allow three months for gloves, umbrellas and the like, and six months for valuables.

Fiddles

From time to time it will become evident that someone is dishonest and checks should be made to ensure that no one is taking advantage of you.

Symptoms of dishonesty include:

- Poor food or liquor gross profit
- Items of food or liquor running out more quickly than they should do
- Items of plant and equipment disappearing or running out quickly
- Employees working in different ways to the procedure manuals
- Restaurant bills going missing
- An over-abundance of 'no sales' on a till role
- Bottles of liquor either full or empty containing brands not normally stocked
- Spirits or beers being watered down
- Lower takings than expected from a particular volume of business
- Employees suddenly carrying supermarket bags in and out of the premises
- Furtive looks from employees as they leave the premises
- Employees suddenly becoming affluent.

Ways of combating dishonesty include:

- Test purchasing in bars and restaurants
- Date stamping bottles before issue to the bar
- Checking empties to ensure that the bottles were stamped
- Security cameras lined up electronically with tills
- Tightening up overall security and management awareness
- Back door searches of bags and locker searches (see page 222)
- Making an example of employees caught thieving
- Setting up regular training in all security matters.

Security of Personnel and Customers

Brian Mumford

In addition to protecting their own property and that of their customers, businesses also have a duty of care for personnel and customers.

Handling emergencies

The management and staff must be prepared to deal with emergencies for they will happen from time to time. The list of possible emergencies is a long one but the most obvious are:

- A fire in the restaurant or kitchen
- A bad cut caused by a knife
- Staff or customer slipping and breaking a bone or knocking head resulting in concussion
- A customer choking on a fish bone
- A customer or member of staff having a stroke, heart attack, epileptic fit
- Loss of water, gas or electricity
- A terrorist bomb threat to the restaurant or in the immediate area.

All members of staff must be instructed about what to do in the case of an emergency and there must be follow-up training from time to time. Some of the precautions are statutory. The Fire Regulations state what should happen with regard to induction and training. There should also be at least one first aider working on the premises. Often it is more important to know what not to do rather than what to do.

It is a good idea to have some portable screens available for emergencies in the restaurant. If the customer cannot be moved they will serve to stop other customers watching what is going on.

There are, of course, other disasters that can befall a business; the answer is to anticipate, have a plan and rehearse it with the staff. Seek expert help as appropriate to ensure that you are doing the right thing.

Incident reports

It is important that allegations by customers of accidents involving injury, loss or damage to their property, or the finding of foreign bodies in food, are fully recorded. Even if the customer makes light of the incident at the time, it does not mean that he or she will not make a claim at some future date. Therefore it is vital that the management of the operation is able to recall exactly what happened at the time.

Unless the details of the allegation and exactly what was said by whom and to whom are recorded, there may only be a vague memory of the details over the passage of time. Should there be a dispute, an investigation by the authorities or a legal claim, much more notice will be taken of on-the-spot reports than of vague memories.

The report should include:

- The name, address and telephone number of the customer involved
- The name and position of the person who dealt with the incident
- The date, time and place of the incident
- A description of the incident
- The value of the articles if appropriate
- The action and decision taken
- Who else was informed.

As a general rule the member of staff should not admit liability for untoward incidents as doing so may influence the decision of the insurance company or the investigating authorities. But it is obviously necessary to try to pacify an irate or excitable customer.

Any correspondence between you and the customer regarding the incident, particularly if you are giving something away as a token of your concern rather than any admittance that it is the fault of the operation, should be headed 'without prejudice'.

Terrorist alert policy

In areas where there may be the possibility of terrorist action, businesses should set up procedures to protect the safety of their staff and customers. This will involve identification of possible suspect objects or packages, and also the procedure to be adopted if there is a specific warning of terrorist acitivity on or near the premises.

Consideration should be given to protecting windows with security film or heavy duty nets as one of the main causes of injury following an explosion is from glass shards which easily pierce the body.

Employees must know what to do in the case of an emergency as indeed they must in the case of fire prevention, fire fighting and evacuation drill. Where possible, the two evacuation drills should be made as similar as possible, so that employees act instinctively. The procedures and drills should be written up and practised.

Management and employees must be continually on the alert for suspect objects and packages but, if the chance of attack is increased, the premises should be systematically searched at least once every hour. If a warning is given and directed at the premises, a search must be made and at the same time it must be decided if customers and employees would be safer to stay where they are or should be moved to another location, either inside or outside the building, always ensuring that the chosen assembly area has been declared safe. Try to avoid car parks or streets with many parked cars.

Management and staff who are likely to answer telephones should also be trained how to handle a caller giving warning of a bomb attack, as vital clues can sometimes be gained by what is said, how it is said and answers to questions asked.

If in doubt about a suspect object or package, do not try to be a hero. Do not touch it, inform the police and evacuate the area.

The police in major cities and towns have published guidelines for businesses in the area on bomb alert policy as well as on the prevention of theft; it is helpful not only to read the guidelines but also to talk to your local police about these issues.

Sample security checklist

TOPIC	DATE	REMARKS
SAFES		
SAFETY DEPOSIT		
BANKING		
CREDIT CONTROL		
REGISTRATION		
CASH CONTROL		
VETTING		
SECURITY TRAINING		
SEARCHES		
LOCKS		
DOOR CLOSERS		
BACK OF HOUSE KEYS		
MASTER KEYS		
PHYSICAL SECURITY	14 Jan 93	All in order
ACCESS CONTROL	14 Jan 93	All in order
LOST AND FOUND PROPERTY		
BARS		
LICENSING		
SAFETY AT NIGHT	14 Jan 93	No problem
INCIDENT REPORTS		
LIAISON WITH POLICE		Good

Signed .... Date ....

Useful Addresses

National telephone dialling codes are given, though local codes may differ. All area codes are due to change on 16 April 1995.

Local councils, tourist boards, Chambers of Commerce and JobCentres can be good sources of help and information. Many organisations listed below will have local offices.

Government departments

Data Protection Registrar
Springfield House, Water Lane, Wilmslow, Cheshire SK9 5AX
Department of Employment
Information Branch, Caxton House, Tothill Street, London SW1H 9NF; 071–273 3000
Department of Health
Information Division, Skipton House, 80 London Road, Elephant and Castle, London SE1 6LW; 071–972 5254
Department of Social Security
Richmond House, 79 Whitehall, London SW1A; 071–210 3000 (or Freefone 0800 666555)
Enterprise Initiative
Freefone 0800 500200 for regional addresses throughout England
Wales: Welsh Office Industry Department, New Crown Buildings, Cathays Park, Cardiff CF1 3NQ; 0222 823976
Scotland: Industry Department for Scotland, Alhambra House, Waterloo Street, Glasgow G2 6AT; 041–248 4774
Ireland: Department of Economic Development, Netherleigh, Massey Avenue, Belfast BT4 2JP; 0232 529900
Last date for applications is 31 March 1994.

HM Customs and Excise
VAT Administration Directorate, New King's Beam House, 22 Upper Ground, London SE1 9PJ; 071–620 1313
Local Enterprise Development Unit (LEDU)
LEDU House, Upper Galwally, Belfast BT8 4TB; 0232 491031
Ministry of Agriculture, Fisheries & Food
Consumer Helpline: Room 303A, Ergon House, c/o Nobel House, 17 Smith Square, London SW1P 3JR; 071–238 6550
Food Science Enquiry Point: Ergon House (address as above); 071–238 6244/45
Mass Helpline: (general contact point on the work of the Ministry and its departments) 10 Whitehall Place West, London SW1A 2HH; 0645 335577 (local call rate)
Office of Fair Trading
Field House, Breams Buildings, London EC4A 1PR; 071–242 2858
Registrar of Companies
Companies House, 55 City Road, London EC1A; 071–253 9393
Companies House, Crown Way, Maindy, Cardiff CF4 3UZ; 0222 388588
Companies House, 102 George Street, Edinburgh EH2 3DJ; 031–225 5774
IDB House, 64 Chichester Street, Belfast BT1 4JX; 0232 234488

Business development
Action for Cities Coordination Unit
Room P2/106, 2 Marsham Street, London SW1P 3EB; 071–276 3053
Development Board for Rural Wales
Ladywell House, Newtown, Powys SY16 1JB; 0686 626965
The Federation of Small Businesses
5th Floor, 114 Union Street, Glasgow G1 3QQ; 041–221 0775
Greater London Business Centre Ltd (formerly London Small Firms Centre)
4th Floor, Bastille Court, No 2 Paris Garden, London SE1 8ND; 071–261 1300 (or Freefone 0800 222999)
Industrial Society
48 Bryanston Square, London W1H 7LN; 071–262 2401
Rural Development Commission
141 Castle Street, Salisbury, Wiltshire SP1 3TP; 0722 336255
Scottish Business Shop
120 Bothwell Street, Glasgow G2 7JP; 041–248 6014
Scottish Enterprise National (for information on LECs in Scotland)
120 Bothwell Street, Glasgow G2 7JP; 041–248 2700
Welsh Development Agency (WDA)
Pearl House, Greyfriars Road, Cardiff CF1 3XX; 0222 222666

Catering industry bodies
Academy of Wine Service
26 Ludlow Road, Guildford, Surrey GU2 5NR; 0483 302373

British Federation of Hotel, Guest House and Self-Catering Associations
5 Sandycroft Road, Blackpool, Lancashire FY1 2RY; 0253 52683
British Hospitality Association
40 Duke Street, London W1M 6HR; 071–499 6641
British Hotels Association (BHA)
40 Duke Street, London W1M 5DA; 071–499 6641
Hotel, Catering and Institutional Management Association (HCIMA)
191 Trinity Road, London SW17 7HN; 081–672 4251
Restaurateurs Association of Great Britain
190 Queens Gate, London SW7 5EU; 071–581 2444

Personnel
Advisory, Conciliation and Arbitration Service (ACAS)
Clifton House, 83–117 Euston Road, London NW1 2RB; 071–396 0022
Commission for Racial Equality
Elliot House, 10–12 Allington Street, London SW1E 5EH; 071–828 7022
Equal Opportunities Commission
Overseas House, Quay Street, Manchester M3 3HN
Health and Safety Executive
Baynards House, 1–13 Chepstow Place, Westbourne Grove, London W2 4TS;
071–229 3456
Institute of Personnel Management (IPM)
IPM House, 35 Camp Road, Wimbledon, London SW19 4UX; 081–946 9100

Training
Hotel and Catering Training Company (HCTC)
International House, High Street, Ealing, London W5 5DB; 081–579 2400
Training and Enterprise Councils (TECs)
England and Wales: 071–273 6969 for all regional offices or ask at your local
JobCentre

Purchasing bodies
HMSO Publications Centre (enquiries)
PO Box 276, London SW8 5DT; 071–873 0011
Purchasing Consortia
Best Western Purchasing, Vine House, 143 London Road, Kingston-upon-
Thames, Surrey KT2 6NA; 081–541 0050
Consort Purchasing, Consort House, 180–182 Fulfers Road, York YO1 4OA;
0904 620137
LMS (Consultants) Ltd, The Old Bakery, South Road, Reigate, Surrey RH2
7LB; 0737 249337
Performing Right Society Ltd
29–33 Berners Street, London W1P 4AA; 071–580 5544

Conversion Charts

Price (value) conversion table

This table is useful to convert the price of goods in metric measure to imperial and vice versa.

Litres to gallons – multiply price × 4.55
Gallons to litres – multiply price × 0.22

Litres to pints – multiply price × 0.57
Pints to litres – multiply price × 1.76

Kilos to pounds – multiply price × 0.45
Pounds to kilos – multiply price × 2.20

Examples:

> If 1 pint costs   27p, a litre will cost:
>   27p × 1.76 = 47.52p

> If 1 kilo costs   56p, a pound will cost:
>   56p × 0.45 = 25.20p

> If 1 gallon costs   £1.50, a litre will cost:
>   £1.50 × 0.22 = 33p

Volume/Weight conversion tables

Multiply the number of litres by 0.22 to give gallons
Multiply the number of gallons by 4.546 to give litres
Multiply the number of litres by 1.76 to give pints
Multiply the number of pints by 0.568 to give litres
Multiply the number of pounds by 0.454 to give kilos
Multiply the number of kilos by 2.205 to give pounds

Examples:

To convert 2 litres into pints:
  2 × 1.76 = 3.52 pints

To convert 3 gallons into litres:
  3 × 4.546 = 13.64 litres

To convert 7 pounds into kilos:
  7 × 0.454 = 3.18 kilos

To convert Centigrade to Farenheit multiply Centigrade by 1.8 and add 32 degrees

To convert Farenheit to Centigrade deduct 32 degrees from Farenheit then multiply by 5 and divide by 9

VAT (value added tax)

VAT is a statutory tax (or sales tax) which is added to the selling price of most retail items – including food and drink sold in hotels and restaurants. The tax is collected from the customer and passed on to the government (Customs and Excise) by the retailer. The rate of tax can vary by Act of Parliament usually announced in the annual Budget Speech by the Chancellor of the Exchequer. Currently, the rate is 17.5 per cent but it can go up or down. The last change was made on 1 April 1991.

To calculate VAT – and calculate the menu price

Method
Multiply the selling price by 17.5 and divide by 100

Example: Selling price of £3.50 – VAT rate 17$^{1}/_{2}$%

  £3.50 ÷ 100 × 17.5 = 61p (VAT)
  £3.50 + 61p = £4.11 (menu price – see below)

Quick method
Multiply the selling price by 1.175 to calculate the menu price

Example: £3.50 × 1.175 = £4.11

How to extract the VAT element from the menu price
Divide the menu price by 6.73 to give the VAT element

Example:
  £4.11 ÷ 6.73 = 61p VAT (£4.11 – 61p = £3.50 = selling price)

Quick method
Divide the menu price by 1.175 to give the selling price (excluding VAT)

Example: £4.11 ÷ 1.175 = £3.50

NB: In this example the 'odd' menu price of £4.11 would probably be increased to £4.15 or £4.25 to make it more 'marketable' on the menu.

A quick method to calculate the approximate selling price using a 'factor' denoting the required %GP

FOR	58%	multiply cost price by factor	2.38
	59%	multiply cost price by factor	2.44
	60%	multiply cost price by factor	2.50
	61%	multiply cost price by factor	2.56
	62%	multiply cost price by factor	2.63
	63%	multiply cost price by factor	2.70
	64%	multiply cost price by factor	2.77
	65%	multiply cost price by factor	2.86
	66%	multiply cost price by factor	2.94
	67%	multiply cost price by factor	3.03
	68%	multiply cost price by factor	3.13
	69%	multiply cost price by factor	3.23
	70%	multiply cost price by factor	3.33
	71%	multiply cost price by factor	3.45
	72%	multiply cost price by factor	3.57
	73%	multiply cost price by factor	3.70
	74%	multiply cost price by factor	3.85
	75%	multiply cost price by factor	4.00

The answer (selling price) is in £p.

Example:

To obtain a %GP of 68% for a dish with a cost price of £1.24 the selling price excluding VAT will be:

£1.24 × 'factor' 3.13 = £3.88

In this case:
The cost is £1.24
The selling price is £4.56 (£3.88 + VAT)
The ex VAT selling price is £3.88
The cash gross profit is £2.64 (£3.88–£1.24)
The percentage gross profit is 68%
The percentage cost of sales is 32%.

Bibliography

Publications

ABC of Licensing Laws, National Licensed Victuallers Association
Hotel and Catering Managers' Guide to the Law, Caterer and Hotelkeeper
Principles of Hotel and Catering Law, 3rd edn, Alan Pannett (Cassell)
Purchasing, Costing and Control, Peter Ogden (Gale Ogden Publications)
Forming a Limited Company, 3rd edn, Patricia Clayton (Kogan Page)
How To Do Your Own Advertising, Michael Bennie (How to Books)
How to Employ and Manage Staff, Peter Taylor (How to Books)
How to Manage People at Work, John Humphries (How to Books)
How to Raise Business Finances, Peter Ibbetson (How to Books)
How to Start a Business From Home, Graham Jones (How to Books)
Hygiene for Management, Richard Sprenger (Highfield Publications)
Kitchen Planning and Management, John Fuller and David Kirt (Butterworth-Heinemann)
Business Law, N Savage (Butterworth)
Financial Management for the Small Business, The Daily Telegraph Guide, 2nd edn, Colin Barrow (Kogan Page)
Law for the Small Business, The Daily Telegraph Guide, 7th edn, Patricia Clayton (Kogan Page)
The Modern Patissier, William Barber (Northwood Publications)
New Larousse Gastronomique (Hamlyn)
Best Wine Buys in the High Street, Judy Ridgway (Foulsham) (published annually)
Working for Yourself: The Daily Telegraph Guide to Self-Employment, 14th edn, Godfrey Golzen (Kogan Page)
Running Your Own Catering Company, Judy Ridgway (Kogan Page)
Marketing Handbook, John Stapleton (Gower)
Market Orientation in the Hotel Industry, Richard Kotas (Surrey University Press)
Principles of Hotel and Catering Law, 3rd edn, Alan Pannett (Cassell)

Government publications

County Courts
Small Claims in the County Court

Department of Employment
Accounting For a Small Firm
Marketing
Starting and Running Your Own Business

HM Customs and Excise
The VAT Guide

HMSO Publications for all government publications such as white papers,
codes of practice (see Useful Addresses)

Inland Revenue
Starting in Business.

Videos and books published by the Hotel Catering and Institutional Management Association (HCIMA)

Support video tapes
Increasing Profitability
Delegation
Improving Communication Skills
Creative Recruiting
Effective Interviewing
Putting the Guest First
Professional Dining Room Service
Better Banquets
Food and Beverage Suggestive Selling
Also various video tapes on sales, training and security

Books
Managing Hospitality Human Resources
Supervision in the Hospitality Industry
Training in the Hospitality Industry
Managing Quality Services
Security and Loss Prevention Management
Managing Bar and Beverage Operations
Managing Service in Food and Beverage Operations
Management of Food and Beverage Operations
Planning Control for Food and Beverage Operations
Purchasing for Hospitality Operations

Managing Hospitality Engineering Systems
Energy and Water Resource Management

Journals

British Hotelier and Restaurateur, 40 Duke Street, London W1M 6HR

Caterer and Hotelkeeper (available weekly on bookstalls), Quadrant House, The Quadrant, Sutton, Surrey SM2 5AS

Catering, 161–165 Greenwich House, Greenwich High Street, London SE10 8JA

Decanter, St John's Chambers, 2–10 St John's Road, London SW11 1PN

Morning Advertiser, The Licensed Victuallers' Association, 13–27 Brunswick Place, London N1 6DX

The Restaurant Magazine (free to restaurant owners and suppliers), Quantum Publishing, 29–31 Lower Coombe Street, Croydon CR9 1LX

Which? Wine Monthly, Consumers' Association, 14 Buckingham Street, London WC2N 6DS

Wine Magazine, 60 Waldegrave Road, Teddington, Middlesex TW11 8LG

List of Advertisers

Index

References in italic indicate figures or tables.